The Strategy of (Re) con

Revisiting India's Multif
Relations with Central

The Strategy of (Re) connectivity

Revisiting India's Multifaceted Relations with Central Asia

Edited by

Kashif Hasan Khan

KNOWLEDGE WORLD

KW Publishers Pvt Ltd
New Delhi

ISBN 978-93-89137-53-8 Hardback
eISBN 978-93-89137-54-5 ebook

Published in India by Kalpana Shukla

KNOWLEDGE WORLD

KW Publishers Pvt Ltd
4676/21, First Floor, Ansari Road
Daryaganj, New Delhi 110002
Phone: +91 11 23263498/43528107
Marketing: kw@kwpub.com
Editorial: production@kwpub.com
Website: www.kwpub.com

Printed and Bound in India

Contents

Foreword

Recently a significant change has taken place through discussions among the leaders of both regions which is undoubtedly lifting "mutual interest" to another level. This is indeed high time for India to deepen its engagement with Central Asia when the relations among the Central Asian states seem to be expanding to levels never seen before. A politically, geographically and economically integrated Central Asia is important for India to achieve its goal of 'connecting' with the region. On the other hand, India the fastest growing economy in the world can also provide benefits to the emerging economies of Central Asia. A policy of projecting India's 'soft power' wherein it assists in capacity building, human resource development, information technology, pharmaceuticals and healthcare, etc., has done tremendously well in the region.

As mentioned repeatedly in the present book that despite many efforts, there is still a need to do much more from both sides. Accepting the fact that there are some highly serious issues like connectivity, the growing influence of China in Central Asia and what that means for India's outreach in the region. China's involvement in key infrastructure projects for a larger strategic purpose like the China-Pakistan Economic Corridor (CPEC) and One Belt and Road Initiative (BRI), if projects focusing on re-connectivity, like the present one, keep coming they will lead to a good end towards ensuring strengthened economic-political relations.

I am thankful to Dr. Kashif Hasan Khan for bringing a very important book on India and Central Asia Relations. The book consists of articles written by scholars from different countries and it is fascinating to have an opportunity to learn different perspectives which can be extremely vital to apprehend the perception of people of different backgrounds.

The contents of the book will surely open up opportunities for young researchers, practitioners and already established academicians. I once again congratulate him and all contributors to finish this great project. I wish a great success!

Dr. Halil Koch
Vice Rector, Ala-Too International University
Bishkek, Kyrgyzstan

Acknowledgements

There are people to whom I am especially indebted and whose assistance has been invaluable completing this publication.

I am particularly grateful to the Rector of Ala-Too International University, Dr. Sanzharbek Erdolatov, and Vice Rector, Dr. Halil Koch for their immense support and encouragement throughout the progress of this project.

I am highly thankful to all contributors from various countries, all experts on Central and South Asia for creating an intellectually stimulating environment and sharing their knowledge to make this book possible. Their thought-provoking ideas will hopefully make this collection of essays drawn from an international conference useful for all those who want to broaden their knowledge on India-Central Asia multifaceted relations and challenges they face.

I also express gratitude to my family for love and support.

I remain grateful to the staff at KW Publishers for their helpfulness during editorial process.

There might have been several lapses and loopholes into our project work but none of the above stated persons or institutions bear any responsibility for any kind of errors. I take full responsibility for any kind of lapses in interpretations and analyses that might have crept into this study.

Kashif Hasan Khan

Notes on Contributors

Prof. Agnieszka Kuszewska is a political scientist, Associate Professor at the Institute of Middle and Far East, Faculty of International and Political Studies, Jagiellonian University in Krakow. She also lectures at Collegium Civitas in Warsaw. She is a member of the European Association for South Asian Studies and Polish Association of International Relations. Her research and teaching focus on international relations, conflict and security studies, political, economic and social challenges of contemporary South and Central Asia. An author of three books and numerous research articles in her field of study, she is also a visiting professor at European, South and Central Asian universities (including Germany, Estonia, Latvia, India, Pakistan, Uzbekistan).

Prof. Ranjana Banerjee is the present Chairperson of the Centre of Russian Studies, Jawaharlal Nehru University, New Delhi. She holds a PhD in literature from Institute of Oriental Studies, Academy of Sciences, Moscow, and a postgraduate degree in Russian Peoples' University (Moscow). She has published her research works in reputed national and international journals and books.

Prof. Halim Nezihoglu is head of Department of International Relations at Ala-Too International University, Bishkek, Kyrgyzstan. His research interests include national identity and ethnic relations in Central Asia. He has published several articles and coordinated national and international conferences.

Prof. Mohd. Sanaullah is a Professor at the Department of Arabic, Aligarh Muslim University, India. He has written over 11 books and 200 plus articles.

Dr. Kashif Hasan Khan is a Director of Silk Road Research Center, Ala-Too International University in Bishkek, Kyrgyzstan. He has previously worked in the corporate sector as an International Business Consultant. He has worked in Turkey, Philippines, England and India. His research and teaching interests include international business, international trade theories, economy of Central Asia and history of economic thoughts. Kashif has written a number of articles, attended and coordinated national and international conferences in India and abroad. His major work has been with ADB (Asian Development Bank), Minorities Commission of India as well as IT sector.

Dr. Sadananda Sahoo is a sociologist, at present an Assistant Professor at the School of Inter-disciplinary and Trans-Disciplinary Studies (SOITS), Indira Gandhi National Open University (IGNOU), New Delhi. He has more than 20 publications and reviews on diaspora and ethnic studies, international migration, public policy, and rural development, among others. Besides, he has also co-edited several books and journals on diasporas, development and education. His recent co-edited book titled "Global Diasporas: Socioeconomic, Cultural and Policy Perspectives" has been published by Springer (2014).

Dr. Poonam Mann is an Associate Fellow at the Centre for Air Power Studies, New Delhi. She specialises in Central Asian studies, and has contributed various articles on the region and presented papers in national and international seminars. She has authored a book titled "India's Foreign Policy in the Post Cold Era."

Dr. Bilal Bhat holds a doctorate degree in sociology from the University of Kashmir, India. He was awarded Post-Doctorate Research Fellowships by the University Grants Commission of India and the Indian Council of Social Science Research, for studying Women Empowerment and Poverty Reduction in Kashmir, and Aspirations and Challenges of Youth in Conflict respectively. He presently works as Assistant Professor in Social Justice.

Dr. Meretguly Gurbanov is a Scientific Expert at the Institute of language and literature named after Magtymguly under the Academy of Sciences of Turkmenistan. He also teaches English language at the languages institute "Diller Dunyasi", Ashgabat, Turkmenistan. His research area includes Hindi and Urdu languages.

The Significance of India's (Re)connectivity Strategy in Central Asia: An Introduction

Agnieszka Kuszewska and Kashif Hasan Khan

India's current geopolitical aspirations as an emerging power call for an in-depth analysis of its strategy of (re)connectivity with resource-rich Central Asia, which New Delhi considers its 'extended neighbourhood'. In the second decade of the 21st century, Central Asia has emerged as a country of paramount geostrategic importance in the 'new Great Game', engaging Russia, China and the United States, all vying over their security and energy related interests in the region. Apart from that, Central Asia has immensely attracted the attention of other significant emerging players such as India, Turkey and Pakistan. For India, Central Asia plays tremendously important role, which has materialised within the scope of 'Connect Central Asia' policy. The rich heritage of multi-layered interconnectivity dating back to the ancient times, civilisational linkages, cultural affinity which characterise India and Central Asia, serve as a valuable background for expanding the ties and exploring the new possible areas of cooperation. Successful implementation of the 'Connect Central Asia' objectives by India will add a new dimension to the relations between these actors. Strategically positioned Central Asia with its rich resources, relatively advanced infrastructure, human capital and recently introduced economic reforms, is an attractive partner for India. Therefore, New Delhi, with its emerging international aspirations, undertakes various initiatives to reconstruct the ancient connections with Central Asia and adjust them to the new geostrategic realities of the 21st century. To what extent would these efforts be successful, and what has to be done to utilize the existing huge potential and fully materialise all benefits of the enhanced inter-regional cooperation, are vital questions this book addresses. It also contextualises the multiple challenges India faces within the framework of the evolving security-related, political and socio-economic factors.

Within the strategy of (re)connectivity, certain prerogatives of the multi-layered partnership cooperation have been initiated by India and Central Asian Republics, but further development of these ties seems to be at halt due to many factors, such as geostrategic specificity of South Asia (protracted conflict with Pakistan, terrorist threat) and lack of direct land route from India to Central Asia. The situation in Afghanistan, especially post-2014 developments with deteriorating security circumstances and growing presence of China in Afghanistan and Central Asia, pose a noteworthy challenge for the government in New Delhi. Conspicuously, India–Central Asia relations must be contextualised within a broad framework of regional geostrategic dynamics and emerging security concerns.

There are a number of security issues of common concern for India and Central Asian Republics, including terrorism, extremism, the situation in Afghanistan, illegal drug trade, etc. Collaboration on promoting peace and security remains one of the crucial tasks in the foreseeable future. The chapters included in this volume discuss multiple geostrategic and security-related issues which are vital to Central Asian states and to India, emphasising the the threats they face, such as terrorism, fundamentalism and their potential consequences. The volume touches upon the China's regional aspirations and objectives, including the massive BRI initiative (Belt and Road), discusses the challenges of (lack of) territorial connectivity between India and Central Asian Republics, the interests of other great powers, etc. Moreover, the book analyses various aspects of legacy of India–Central Asia connectivity with its historical background and contextualises the discourse within the scope of a larger regional complex, while thoroughly referring to the contemporary strategic, socio-political and economic dynamics. The strategy of (re)connectivity is viewed in geopolitical terms as well as in cultural terms. All in all, the volume is a contribution to the literature on contemporary regional and global strategic shifts and challenges in South and Central Asia and beyond, as it focuses on emerging dimensions, multiple regional implications of inter-regional (re)connectivity and cooperation.

The contributors' initial assumption that India and Central Asian Republics had great civilisational contacts in history, paves the way to detailed analysis. Due to its strategic location, demographic configuration and accessibility of oil and mineral wealth, Central Asia has become critical for worldwide politics. Bordered by Russia, Afghanistan, Iran and China, Central Asia is located in the centre of geostrategic rivalries, ongoing conflicts, ambitious actors willing to control their spheres of influence. Lack of direct land connection remains India's major disadvantage vis-à-vis Russia and China. Following the breakdown of the USSR in 1991, other players, including the United States as a sole superpower, enhanced its position in Central Asia. Even when India assumed its position as a rising power, it did not have very specific policies towards Central Asian Republics (CAR's). At the turn of the centuries India was undergoing economic transformation and was focused on the implementation of the relevant reforms. However, in the last two decades India has embraced a very proactive approach and has made the region part of its 'extended neighbourhood'.

The volume discusses trade exchange and relationship between India and Central Asian Republics. The CAR's region has massive amounts of energy resources, which could positively contribute to face India's energy requirements and consequently, sustain its relatively high economic growth. Both complement each other for sizeable manpower and markets. CAR's have a huge consumer market for a range of goods and services. India has the ability to provide support to develop Central Asians' capacities in areas such as information technology, knowledge industries and soft power. In the Cold War era, the Indian Technical and Economic Cooperation (ITEC), one of the several initiatives towards strengthening the relationship, started in 1964 as a form of bilateral assistance and capacity building through training programs, study tours, technology transfers and, in some cases, aid for disaster relief. This tradition of cooperation should be further expanded and improved. In recent years India has identified a number of new sectors in which it has considerable strength for cooperation: automobile industry, textiles, hotels, banking and insurance, drugs and pharmaceuticals. India has also offered facilities for training of Central Asian Journalist, diplomats and students through ITEC Program. India-CAR's bilateral trade may be small in volume, yet it has been growing steadily over the years and holds potential for growth and diversification. Merging these goals and interests provides an enhanced chance to bring together the main producers and consumers.

This volume is especially focused on the current challenges and opportunities the regions face. Despite the goodwill that ITEC programs and scholarships have generated, this has failed to translate into substantive trade and commercial relations between India and Central Asia. India still struggles to boost bilateral/multilateral cooperation with Central Asian states. Prime Minister Narendra Modi's visit to all five Republics in 2015 is considered as one of the most significant steps taken by India towards strengthening the ties with this region. It not only enhanced the 'Connect Central Asia' policy initiated by then Prime Minister Dr. Manmohan Singh in 2012, but also embarked upon new policies which initiated building Chabahar Airport in Iran that came chiefly due to the failure of TAPI (Turkmenistan-Afghanistan-Pakistan-India) project. A large number of top ministers and bureaucrats have visited each other's countries since 2015. The strategy of (re)connectivity continues to expand high-level political interactions on bilateral and multilateral forums, extending trade and economic cooperation, military training, joint research, counter terrorism, multilateral engagement.

The contributors touch upon another crucial factor, i.e. security challenges, in their respective chapters. As highlighted above, despite shared concerns over security, the security ties between India and Central Asian states still need considerable work. Whereas Russia conducts numerous joint military exercises with these states under the framework of the Commonwealth of Independent (CIS) and Collective Security Treaty Organization, and China does to some degree through the SCO (Shanghai Cooperation Organization), there is limited direct collaboration with India's armed forces. However, it is doubtful that India will be able to utilize the SCO platform to advance its own given the predominant Chinese influence within the organization and Beijing's sensitivity towards Pakistan, which is also an observer in the SCO. With the creation of the SCO in 2001, China has already gained acceptance as a major economic and security partner that plays a stabilising role in Central Asia. Compared to India's trade turnover of $366.73 million with Central Asia in 2008, Iran's was nearly $1.8 billion and China's exceeded $28.18 billion. China's more recent approach has been to increase its influence in the region via greater economic engagement. The SCO has been especially helpful in this regard by roping Russia into a cooperative framework. The pipeline from Turkmenistan via Uzbekistan and Kazakhstan to China is symbolic of China's growing economic thrust into the region. Pakistan has always occupied a central place in India's foreign policy. The dynamic situation in Central Asia offers opportunities to Pakistan to enhance its strategy relying on Islamic fraternity, which New Delhi considers anti-India. This is a matter of deep concern for Indian policy makers. Due to economic alignment, strategic scenario and fragile political setup, Central Asia is considered as a very significant area by the outside powers including India. It makes imperative for India to look towards this area with more seriousness due to its geo-economic and geo-strategic implications. Narendra Modi, elected for the second term as India's Prime Minister, will certainly undertake multiple initiatives aimed at strengthening India's international position, providing economic growth, attracting investments, diversifying strategic resources, enhancing 'extended neighbourhood' policy. There is a great deal of focus on joint ventures, investments, because infrastructure is being developed in all these countries. The Central Asian Republics have enormous hydrocarbon reserves: 90 to 200 billion oil barrels and gas 46 per cent known world gas reserves. The CAR's strategic goal is to diversify their economies and develop new partnerships to enhance economic, security-related, political and socio-cultural cooperation. Central Asia has the potential not only to emerge as an important energy provider to India, but to define its international identity as a separate geostrategic entity. The coming years will undoubtedly play an important role in this endeavour and it is in India's interest to participate actively in Central Asia's enhanced connectivity with major international actors.

This book aims to provide a better understanding of India–Central Asia's multi-faceted relations in rapidly evolving geostrategic dynamics. It serves as a timely insight into the contours of India and Central Asian states' policies, emerging trends and significant features of these interactions. The chapters are authored by academics and researchers from India, Central Asia and Europe, to provide a wide spectrum of opinion and analysis with regard to the subject. In April 2019, the

Ala-Too International University in Bishkek, Kyrgyzstan, organised an International Conference titled 'India and Central Asian Relations: Economic, Historical and Cultural Perspectives'. The event was held in collaboration with University of Hyderabad in Telangana, India and American University of Central Asia in Bishkek, Kyrgyzstan. This volume is an outcome of academic deliberations, exchange of views and ideas between the experts and contains the papers subsequently submitted by renowned scholars with expertise on South and Central Asia.

In the opening chapter, 'China's Belt and Road Initiative: Comparative Perspectives on India and Central Asia', Sadananda Sahoo points out that Belt and Road initiative is an ambitious plan to interlink many Asian countries with the leadership of China. The chapter examines the impact of BRI on Asian countries in general and provides a comparative perspective on India and Central Asia in particular. The author debates on consequences on both smaller countries such as Central Asia and the big powers such as India, and analyses two broad scenarios that will affect the border communities, considering the complexities of South Asian countries and its history and the present-day political-economy: (i) Escalation of conflict between two major powers such as India and China and hence further marginalisation of the border communities; (ii) Successful completion of OBOR project through negotiation and peaceful understanding resulting in mainstreaming the border communities.

In the chapter 'Prospects, Threats and Challenges of India's "Connect Central Asia" Policy in the Current International Security Context', Agnieszka Kuszewska emphasises the necessity to study the policy and challenges of re(connectivity) between India and Central Asia and explores the challenges of 'Connect Central Asia' policy in today's rapidly evolving and dynamic regional security environment. The current international security context relates to the threats and challenges India faces, including protracted conflict with Pakistan, unstable situation in Afghanistan, concerns regarding China's aspirations. The primary research objective of this chapter is to study both prospects and limitations of India's enhanced security-related and economic cooperation with CAR's. The analysis of the India–Central Asia relations from the perspective of the Central Europe-based researcher may shed light on the new perception of inter-regional cooperation in Asia as a whole, and India's role in the contemporary world in particular. The methodological framework is based on an in-depth, multidisciplinary and quality research carried out in South and Central Asia as well as in Europe.

Poonam Mann's chapter 'India's Connectivity Push and Road to Central Asia' refers to Halford J. Mackinder's 'Heartland Theory' which emphasised Central Asia's geostrategic significance in the regional and global power game. The geostrategic centrality and role of Iran as a facilitator in India–Central Asia Cooperation is put into an in-depth analysis. Iran is without any doubt one of the key engaging points for India in New Delhi's attempts to re(connect) Central Asia. Efficient cooperation offers tremendous economic opportunities to all participants – CAR's, India, Iran and Afghanistan, which is a prerequisite of peace, security stability and sustainable socio-economic development.

In his chapter, 'The Importance of India for Multi-Vector Foreign Policy of Kyrgyzstan', Halim Nezihoglu argues that Central Asia became an arena for great power rivalry, a 'new great game', after the dissolution of the Soviet Union. The region's geopolitical importance, rich energy resources, strategic considerations and regional rivalry, motivated great powers to take the benefits of new opportunities. Unlike other powers, India never pursued an imperialist policy in the region and may counterbalance the hegemonic aspirations of other great players in Central Asia. Central Asian republics have pursued multi-vectorism as their general foreign policy orientation, and tried to develop its ties with different countries. Focusing on Kyrgyzstan the author concludes that strengthening relations with India might be an important alternative option for foreign policy orientation of Kyrgyzstan as well for its peaceful political development, stable transition and social progress.

Bilal Bhat in his chapter titled 'Milieu of National Initiatives: Perspective on Cross Leveraging India and Central Asia Relations- A Case Study of Uzbekistan' points out that the dawn of self-governing free nations in Central Asia obliged redefining and restructuring of Indo-Central Asian affairs. India has numerous recompenses to expand socio-economic and socio-political ties with Central Asian Countries for having geographical proximity, historical ties, culture and tradition besides age-old economic and political connections. The author's field experience of Uzbekistan delineated the scope of India and Central Asian countries cooperation for reasons of historical and socio-cultural ties. Lack of skilled manpower, sophisticated technology and marketization are a strapping impediment in the utilization of existing natural capital in Central Asia. India with increased professional manpower and technological advancement can play a very vital role in harnessing the available resources. Besides, there is a growing interest amongst young and old about Indian educational system, cinema, economy, political system and other socio-cultural patterns of life. The peoples of Central Asia are very much aware of the Indian culture, and appreciate its movies, music and dances. Unfortunately, as the author points out, not very many Indians know about modern Central Asian Republics. The author highlights the lack of emphasis on teaching about other cultures in schools and non-governmental institutions, and the shortage of other sources of information. He touches upon some facets of relationship based on his personal observations and experiences.

Mohd. Sanaullah's chapter 'Khwaja Bakhtiyar Kaki of Osh (1173–1235) and the Indo-Kyrgyz Sufi-trajectory' discusses the historic heritage of connectivity between the Indian subcontinent and Central Asia, by thoroughly describing the activities of a revered Sufi saint, Khwaja Bakhtiyar Kaki of Osh (presently in Kyrgyzstan). He points out that Muslim theology, culture and politics of medieval India owe much to Fergana valley, which stands central to the Sufi-trajectory of the Indian subcontinent. Chishtiya and Naqshbandiya orders are linked to the valley in their early stages. Khwaja Qutbuddin Bakhtiar Oshi Kaki was a spiritual master of Baba Farid Ganj-e-Shakar, one of the most revered Punjabi preachers and mystics. The author analyses the state patronage of the Sufis during Delhi Sultanate. As a patron saint of Delhi, Kaki enjoyed prestige and authority, and influenced the Sultan's style of governance.

Ranjana Banerjee's chapter 'South, East and Central Asia: A Dialogue of Cultures through Silk Route' focuses on the various, historically inherited cultural encounters, which took place in the form of borrowing, adaptation, assimilation, dissemination along the Silk Route, specifically South, East and Central Asia. The author provides an in-depth study of the commonalities and specificities traced in art and architecture, culinary, legends and tales. The cross-cultural affinities and linkages provide an excellent and crucial element of the (re)connectivity challenges in the relations between Central Asia and India.

Meretguly Gurbanov's in the chapter titled 'Historical Bonds and Common words between Hindi (Urdu) and Turkmen' refers to the historical bonds between Turkmenistan and India and provides an analysis of Urdu/Hindi and Turkmen languages and their common words based on historical documents. The author takes account of the fact that India offered a fertile environment for famous Turkmen commanders, scholars and poets while being the source of inspiration. Consequently, the linkages were enormous and contributed to shaping the historical dynamics of the two regions. He describes some great Turkmen scholars who visited and worked in the Indian Subcontinent, such as Al-Beruni, who learnt Sanskrit and wrote The History of India. Another prominent poet inspired by Hindustan was Magtymguly Pyragy who is considered the greatest Turkmen spiritual leader, philosopher and Sufi poet, renowned for his efforts to unite the Turkmen nation.

The above enumerated chapters touch upon several contexts, including political challenges, economic interactions, social relations, linguistics, etc., in order to come up with a wide-ranging understanding of the two regions. Consequently, the aim of this volume is to help the readers/ policymakers to have an in-depth analysis of the region from different perspectives and its growing significance in contemporary international relations. The book addresses several pressing issues, such as bilateral cooperation, current security threats and their potential consequences.

The scientific analysis offered here can be helpful for framing the future policies by India and Central Asian Republics, to provide comprehensive solutions to vital challenges and act as an inspiration for an ongoing debate among the researchers, policymakers, academics, journalists, etc. According to the authors it is of utmost importance to enhance the significance of in-depth studies focusing on the (re)connectivity strategy of India with reference to specific sectors, the Central Asian region as a whole and particular Central Asian states, and on comprehensive analysis of India's growing presence in Central Asia and beyond.

In 1995 Narasimha Rao, the then India's Prime Minister, emphasised during his visit to Turkmenistan: 'We are an independent partner with no selfish motives. We only desire honest and open friendship and to promote stability and cooperation without causing harm to a third country' (Kothari, Raj Kumar: 2018). It could have been sketched from the words of Rao that after the plunge of USSR the economic cooperation was a driving force behind India's objective of enhanced engagement with Central Asia. Today the strategic situation has drastically changed, with enhanced security threats from Pakistan-based terrorist groups and war-torn Afghanistan. However, the core content of Rao's words remains unchanged: India aims to provide a win-win cooperation based on partnership exchange. Being a democracy in contrast to other regional powerful players, India apparently has the largest potential to implement an equality- and values-based policy, adhering to impressive historical heritage and unprecedented cultural ties with Central Asia. Taking this into consideration, India emerges as a natural ally of Central Asian Republics in their quest for new geostrategic position and identity.

policy, conflict resolution, international relation, media engagement etc. Considering all complexities, this paper tries to provide some policy input for making the project viable and sustainable.

Fig 1.1: The Belt and Road Initiative: Six Economic Corridors Spanning Asia, Europe and Africa

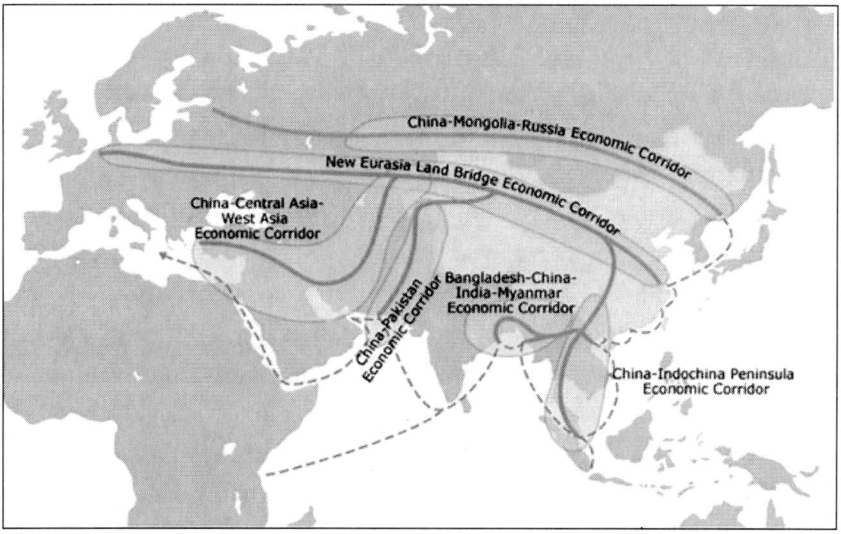

Source: http://china-trade-research.hktdc.com

BRI Map

Transnational infrastructural projects have played a key role in transmission of goods, services, people and cultures from one part of the world to another. The process heralded by geographical exploration in the 15th century and the subsequent colonisation by European nations continues unabated. The process of globalisation has further given boost to the process of 'global village' and 'networked communities'. Historically, the construction of Panama Canal, Suez Canal and Trans-Siberian Railways not only facilitated the material transportation but also turned out to be a network of ideological and cultural transmission.

While 'economy' and 'economical' propositions are the backbones of transnational projects, it is not without self-interest, conflict and ideological wars. The levels of control, tolerance and permissibility along the international trade route often determine the feasibility of such projects.

China's One Belt One Road (BRI) project, while taking into account trade implications and economic value, has yet to delve into its possible impact on Asian countries. There are also possibilities of regional flare-ups on issues related to ethnicity, resource sharing and political interest.

The New World System BRI?

With the dominance in Trade and Commerce and new infrastructure projects such as BRI, there is possibility of a new world system shaping up with the leadership of China. It's not by accident that the rise of global superpowers has coincided, in various periods, with mastering and controlling the transport and communication networks. While Romans, famed for their road construction, enjoyed their superiority over land transport, a similar power play was witnessed in Asia during the ancient times when China had a major say in controlling the Silk Road. From the 16th to 19th century, it was the European colonial powers, English, Dutch, Portuguese and French, dominating the sea warfare, and thus ultimately the naval routes. A similar analogy was embedded for the 21st century with aerial supremacy, not by controlling the aerial routes but by mastering the aerial power, in which the US unarguably came to play a dominating role. The rise of the US as an economic and hegemonic power is being challenged, if not openly, than covertly by China, which has been expanding its economic tentacles across continents.

The BRI project could be seen in a similar light—as an attempt to explore, exploit and integrate the nation-state markets along the ancient Silk Road for the economic well-being and sustainability of China's growing economy. Juxtaposing the proposed BRI with the functional value of ancient Silk Route provides us some insight, which is valuable as well as discernible. While the ancient Silk Road developed naturally and organically over the centuries, the BRI, on the other hand, is meticulously planned with economic concern at the heart of its man-made modernistic design. During the ancient times, Chinese silk was the most precious commodity of trade. So much so that in absence of foreign exchange, it came to occupy a central currency value on the basis of which other commodities were exchanged and bartered. In today's time, Chinese consumer goods may not have the same notional value like silk, but are ubiquitous in its presence and are widely consumed globally.

One of the distinct features of the BRI is somewhat ironically its inherent ambiguity. According to the report "One Belt, One Road: An Economic Roadmap", "The official document tends to paint the initiative in broad brushstrokes, providing more by way of general conceptualisations than detailed specifics. This invite (ed) open interpretation as to what exactly the programme entails. The original term, the Silk Road Economic Belt and 21st Century Maritime Silk Road, repeats "Silk Road" twice. As that suggests, the initiative's main inspiration comes from the ancient caravan routes that once connected imperial China to the world outside."

The Ancient Silk Route was a civilisation network, which connected China, India, Persia, Greek and Rome and had far-reaching consequences. It was also the genesis and cradle of Chinese dispersal which energised the ancient trade route. The Chinese traders and merchants flourished and paved the way for great Chinese Diaspora and 'sojourning' along with other ethnic groups en route to China, India, Arabia to Asia Minor and Southern Europe. The border communities along the transport network were the first to get exposed to multiculturalism–diverse cultures, religions, languages and material goods and artefacts. The construction of Caravanserais along the Silk Route, which provided resting houses to travellers and traders turn out to be a meeting point of ideas and cultures as Peter Frankopan in The Silk Roads: A New History of the World argues: "There was a good reason why the cultures, cities and people who lived along the Silk Road developed and advanced: as they traded and exchanged ideas, they learnt and borrowed from each other, stimulating further advances in philosophy, the sciences, the language and religion. Progress was essential, as one of the rulers of the kingdom of Zhao in northeastern China at one extremity of Asia more than 2,000 years ago knew all too well. 'A talent for following the ways of yesterdays,' declared King Wu-ling in 307 BC, "is not sufficient to improve the world of today.' Leaders in the past understood how important it was to keep up with the times." (Frankopan, P., 2015). In contrast to Silk Route, BRI is clearly of economic interest to China, since China gave special protection to it during the post-Maoist revolution. This is true for Chinese border communities and traders who traversed different parts of the world. For them, it was their business interest, which mattered more than politics. Robin Cohen (2008) while talking about Chinese Diaspora during colonial times delineates the chief attributes of such communities, which is centred on business rather than the nation-state.

"The Chinese traders had ambivalent attitudes both to the colonial powers and to their place of settlement.... they were loyal to thriving entrepots and profitable arrangements, not caring over much whether the British, French, Portuguese, Malays, Dutch or Indians were in charge of the political superstructure...the lack of commitment to local political life in the places of which the Chinese migrated was linked to the practice of sojourning rather than settling." The Chinese sojourning and other such communities could easily be called as border communities, which emerge with flourishing trade at the borderland.

The highly mechanised and automated construction of BRI is likely to provide the much-needed trans-national movement of people who would be constructing, managing, maintaining and operationalising the new trade route with possible impact on these communities. The magnitude of BRI's impact could be gauged from the fact, as Amiya Chandra in The Trade Game: Engaging with Central Asia, says: "The project will involve 65 countries with a total population reach 4.4 billion and share of global economy of 30 per cent. It's more than 7 times larger than America's Marshall Plan to rebuild Europe after the Second World War"

The BRI initiative has been as much an economic move as political. Chinese President Xi Jinping while announcing it in 2013 at Astana said, "For more than 2000 years, the people who live in the region that connects east and west have been able to coexist, co-operate and flourish despite differences in race, belief and cultural background... it's a 'foreign policy priority' for China to develop friendly co-operative relations with the Central Asian countries. The time has come for a 'Silk Road Economic Belt' to be built - in other words, a New Silk Road."

Impact on border and marginal communities

There are few cases of transnational project like BRI, barring probably trans-Siberian railway network, which could afford us a glimpse into their impact on border communities. Mega infrastructural projects like Panama and Suez Canals had their impact on ethnic communities in the region. Incidentally, both these projects were a meeting point for transnational trade and commerce. The Panama Canal, which was opened in 1914, significantly reduced the international shipping routes, but was responsible for destroying the natural ecosystem of the region. It led to deforestation, pollution and water scarcity and ecological imbalance and was also responsible for regional climate change. Socially and culturally it "displaced twenty-one known communities at the time, and degraded the landscape for those communities that were able to remain on the periphery of the Canal" (The Economist, 2016).

Culturally, "American political and economic interests brought to Panama racist perspectives of tropical societies and cultures not uncommon in the imperialist early-1900s; perspectives deployed and activated to justify the exploitation of the Panamanian people and environment."(The Economist, 2016). The same study observed that, known for its dual economy, Panama faced the internal conflict as Canal operated as a "dynamic, high-wage, export-oriented segment" and the rest of Panama as a rigid, low-earning, domestic-oriented segment" (The Economist, 2016). It is a documented fact that hundreds of workers died because of malaria during the construction of the canal. Quoting David McCullough study (1977) "The Path Between the Seas: The Creation of the Panama Canal 1870- 1914" Sarah Rhoads (2012) mentioned that there were 5,609 deaths throughout the construction (Rhoads: 2012; 64). In addition to the human casuality which is the direct result of construction, there are so many environmental health risks too.

The environmental health risks of increased traffic at the Canal were widespread, as studies have pointed out. "Ships are a major contributor to air pollution, which is concentrated in port communities where ships idle for days as they unload." One study suggests, "Ship emissions may cause as many as 60,000 deaths a year worldwide from heart disease and cancer" (The Economist, 2016).

The 'new Panama Canal' launched by the Nicaraguan government in 2013, which became operational in 2016 offers a good example into the Chinese-operated project. The project linked the Pacific and the Caribbean through a 278 kilometre-long canal, which was three times the length of the original and twice as wide and deep than its prototype. Built by Hong Kong Nicaragua Canal Development Group (HKND), the project witnessed wide protest and slogans like "Chinese, get out" and "No Canal" caught the imagination of local people. The project impacted the Rama and Kriol peoples who had inhabited the area. Over 52 per cent of the planned route passed through their traditional homeland.

It has been argued that the Nicaraguan government did not take local people into confidence before the project was planned and executed. It destroyed some 4,000 square kilometres of tropical forest and swamps as the "Chinese company surveying the planned route, (were) accompanied by the army, police and the Nicaragua's Attorney General." According to a report prepared by Humboldt Centre, some 282 settlements and 24,100 houses were destroyed and some 119,000 people were displaced.

The construction of Suez Canal was another mega navigational project that revolutionised the naval route. It shortened the journey between North Atlantic and northern Indian Oceans via the Mediterranean and Red seas by almost 7,000. It had more commercial value than the social and environmental cost. A report by middleeasteye.net (2015) mentioned that the "recent construction of 45-mile bypass, dubbed the "new Suez Canal" by the Egyptian government, is said to have displaced some 2,000 Egyptians and over 1,000 residential buildings were destroyed. Agricultural lands were confiscated, with no compensation or alternate housing provided"to the displaced masses.

If we look into the annual progress report of BRI, it has followed the much-predicted lines of progression. The first stage was invariably a euphoric expectation because of its newness, followed by critical evaluation and apprehension and finally the realistic realisation of its importance and the incurring costs and benefits. Add to these, national interests of the nations involved in the project and its relationships with countries that carry the flagship of the project. More often than not, historical precedence and prejudices have played a significant role in the formation of perception in the respective nations. It is no wonder that the BRI project, while progressive in its endeavour, is also mired in controversies. Not because of its inherent weaknesses or possibility of a disruptive game-changer but because of the fact that countries have to view it in their self-interest vision.

A large number of national governments are viewing the BRI project as China's imperialistic design (Colucci, Lamont: 2017) to further its trading interests, which involves participation of some 68 countries and 65 per cent of the world population. It is being argued that BRI will impact the sovereignty and territorial sharing of the countries involved. Some have suggested that it better be managed by consortium of nations instead of China taking the initiative and calling the shot. The recent controversial deals of China in Sri Lanka, Pakistan and Nepal and Maldives, where it has invested heavily, has come under sharp attack because of its attempt to infiltrate into the host countries' economy.

Lately some section of Pakistan has been critical and apprehensive of China's role in its economic affair and has viewed China's attempt as seeking a foothold on its soil (Chaudhury: 2018). The US and India, on the other hand, have come to reflect their respective governments' concern as the proposed BRI passes through Pakistani-administered Kashmir, which is considered a disputed area by India. It has been claimed that what China is doing is part of its 'Peripheral Diplomacy' to wield indirect economic influence in the South Asian countries.

Although such claims and counterclaims are part of any trans-national projects, a larger picture on the project is yet to emerge, as it is just the beginning of the mega project and China has not gone beyond Pakistan. It is yet to be seen how other Central and Western Asian, or for that matter European nations, respond to the project. If China wants to succeed in its ambitious project, it has no better alternate but to take the stakeholders in its confidence and draw a detail road map of the project, taking into consideration the concern and reservation of its partners.

The genesis of BRI project could be contextualised with the rising, but irreversible wave of trans-border movement of capitals, the growing globalization and an increase in borderless international trade. The increasing volume of cement and steel production in China has further intensified search for newer geographical areas where these produce could be consumed to keep China's economy growing. China's economic growth rate of 6.8 per cent in the first quarter of 2018 and that of European Union at 2.3 per cent in 2018 offers a glimpse into the yawning deficit between the two regions. The BRI project will not only impact the border communities of Central Asia and European Union but will have an indirect influence by creating material and manpower demand in these regions. But the supply of skilled manpower from border communities are often not fulfilled and such projects are forced to import such manpower from the easily available and cheap suppliers. The process was evidently noticed during the colonial periods when colonial powers moved people from one part of the world to another for the construction of road and railway networks. In the case of BRI, the manpower deficit is to be filled in by countries manning the project, in this case obviously the China. Nonetheless, as BRI is a long-term project, a concerted afford could be made from the very beginning to empower the border communities by providing them employment, making them a stakeholder in the project, imparting training for the relevant skills.s

Conflicts in South Asia

Conflict is one of the most important reason for the under development of the South Asian region. "South Asia is the second most violent place on earth after Iraq. While conflicts in Afghanistan and Pakistan have attracted global attention, parts of India, Sri Lanka, and Nepal have also experienced long-running conflict. The result is human misery, destruction of infrastructure and social cohesion, and death. The knock-on effects are huge" (Ghani & Iyer: 2010). Lack of intra-regional cooperation, a not so vibrant economy and low level of skills further deteriorate the situation and escalate conflicts. In this context, any big infrastructural project such as BRI may lead to disengagement from the prevailing conflict and make way for productive engagement. The vicious cycle of conflict and lack of development makes the region one of the most vulnerable in the world.

The Rohingya crisis in Burma and the refugee crisis in Assam, India, further intensified the conflict in the region as it directly affects the bordering South Asian countries especially Bangladesh and India. In fact, it has been a major political issue for Bangladesh and India in recent times.

Central Asia

Central Asia is geographically a large area, and a compact and landlocked region within the Eurasian landmass. The region contained only two countries, i.e. Mongolia and Afghanistan till 1991. The breakup of USSR or Soviet Union added few more independent countries to the region. There are Lowland Population and Subsistence Patterns. Most Central Asia's desert inhabitants live in narrow belt where the mountains meet the basins and plains. Most of the counties have a past experience in Soviet communist rule. However, in recent times there is a growing presence of China across central Asian region. In fact, after China reemerged as a unified country in 1949, it reclaimed most of its old Central Asian territories. A map of Central Asia follows.

Fig 1.2: The Caucasus and Central Asia

Source: http://www.maps-of-the-world.net/maps-of-asia/

Conflict vis-à-vis political economy of Central Asia

Historically Central Asia has experienced few ethnic conflicts: (1) War in Tajikistan in 1991 over ethnic conflicts; (2) Invasion of Azerbaijan by Armenia; (3) Conflict in Afghanistan which is adjacent to three central Asian countries such as Turkmenistan, Tajikistan and Uzbekistan. In May 1992, political and social tensions in the former Soviet Republic of

Tajikistan escalated to a devastating civil war, which killed approximately 40,000-100,000 people and displaced more than one million (Epkenhans: 2016). The claims regarding the number of deaths are still contested; however, there is no denying the fact that the conflict increased during the period 1992 to 1997.

The ethnic groups from the Garm and Gorno-Badakhshan regions of Tajikistan, who were underrepresented in the ruling elite, revolted against the national government of President Rahmon Nabiyev. The conflict ended with the signing of the "General Agreement on the Establishment of Peace and National Accord in Tajikistan" and the "Moscow Protocol". The next major conflict in Central Asia was in 2010—the clashes between ethnic Kyrgyz and Uzbeks in southern Kyrgyzstan, primarily in the cities of Osh and Jalal-Abad, in the aftermath of the ouster of former President Kurmanbek Bakiyev on April 7. There have been periodic conflicts in Tajikistan between rebel and government forces. The situation might have improved now.

Kyrgyzstan has also exhibited increasing authoritarianism under President Akaev in recent years. Nervous about the rise of Islamicism in the country, combined with the effect of Islamic Movement of Uzbekistan (IMU) incursions in 1999 and 2000, Akaev's government has been cracking down on Islamist movements and groups, but it has also imprisoned members of the opposition (Oliker. et al.: 2003).

The combination of a weak economy, widespread poverty, and increasing autocracy is a dangerous one. In this context, the potential for ethnic conflict also cannot be overlooked, especially as it overlaps with the religious dimension (Oliker et al.: 2003).

Another study by Swanström, N.L.P. et al. (2005) identified that the conflict potential exists in the region along a number of conflict lines. Ethnicity, regionalism, resources, government, religion, and organised crime are the most apparent conflict lines.

Various studies (Oliker: 2003; Swanström: 2005; Epkenhans: 2016) in the region indicate that the potential areas of conflict may be due to three major reasons: (1) power transition from the authoritarian rule (2) the rising gap between the rich and poor and (3) Islamisation

The Central Asian countries predominantly depend on oil, gas, cotton, gold and metals. Countries like Kazakhstan, Turkmenistan and Uzbekistan have formed their development paths around a combination of these resources, especially oil and gas. However, the industries by exploiting the resources, employment and skill generation and global connectivity will definitely help in making these countries reduce conflict.

Political economy of India

Since independence, India's economy was based on socialist-inspired policies, i.e. state-ownership of various sectors, regulation and red tape which was known as 'Licence Raj' and protection from the world markets. However, India opened to the market-based economy, which is broadly termed as liberalisation, only in 1990s. Today, India is one of the fastest growing among the large economies and it is a country run by democracy. New Delhi positioned itself as the world's fifth-largest economy and shortly overtook France. Its GDP growth is about 6 per cent. India's economy is projected to be the world's second-largest, behind only China by 2050.

Demographically India is home to 1.36 billion people, i.e about 17 per cent of the world's population according to World Population Review (2019). Besides, it has the world's largest youth population though the potential demographic dividend has not yet been utilised. Over 30 per cent of India's youth are NEETs (not in employment, education or training), according to the OECD. Overall, India positions itself as a strong Asian power only next to China.

BRI and India

India so far is not part of the BRI. However, with the other Asian countries joining the project it may join at a later stage if the project shows feasibility. India's apprehensions are mainly due to China's expansionism and growing military presence in the region. The recent 2017 China–India border standoff or Doklam standoff between the Indian Armed Forces and the People's Liberation Army of China over Chinese construction of a road in Doklam near a tri-junction border area is already known. Though it is diffused for the time being, it may have the potential for future conflict.

India and Central Asia: A Comparative Perspective

Central Asia that includes Kazakhstan, Kyrgyzstan, Tajikistan, Turkmenistan, and Uzbekistan has a population of about 70 million and stretches from the Caspian Sea in the west to China in the east and from Afghanistan in the south to Russia in the north. India has almost the same population as China. However, the rise of China provides both opportunity as well as vulnerability in the region in many ways. The BRI is one of the biggest venture of recent times which has the potential to alter the political economy in the entire region by interconnecting the natural resources, industrial zones and many other potential hubs that have economic and political significance.

Opportunities

- Use of natural resources: As mentioned earlier many Central Asian regions have underutilised natural resources such as oil and minerals. With the BRI these can be connected with the larger hubs through port as well as road network. Significantly China has been increasingly investing in this region for preparing a large economic hub in the future.
- Migration: With the construction of BRI there will be an increasing flow of capital from one side and labour/human mobility on the other. A considerable share of the economically active population of the Central Asian countries is working abroad, i.e. in Uzbekistan and Russia, Kazakhstan or a Western country. With the BRI such migration will certainly intensify both within the Central Asian region and abroad. Kazakhstan also has the world's largest reserves of zinc, lead and chromite. This may emerge as an industrial hub and further impact the migration in the region. Turkmenistan is rich in natural gas with almost 5 per cent of the world's natural gas.
- Employment: With the increased trade, investment and tourism there are huge possibilities of employment in a diverse range of areas. The increased manufacture in several areas where natural resource are abundant can lead to the local employment as the supply chain become active.
- Tourism: Another major area which is unexploited due to the conflicts and connectivity in the region is tourism. This is one of

the major employment generating activities fuelling other activities in manufacturing, agriculture and service sectors. In these times of global uncertainty, equitable employment is essential to increasing social inclusion, peace and security. The World Economic Forum Report (2016) identified tourism, travel and hospitality as one of the sectors with the highest potential. This sector continues to grow and stay resilient despite global challenges. The report states that tourism provides 10 per cent of the world's GDP, 7 per cent of global trade and as many as one in every 11 jobs globally (ILO: In each of the six years following the global economic crisis of 2010, the number of international tourist arrivals around the world grew by 4 per cent or above.

- Reduce Trade cost

These five areas are very important to the overall development of the region. BRI has potential to influence positively.

Vulnerability

Most of the Central Asian countries are still weak economically as well as politically. After the breakup of former USSR, the Central Asian region went through an economic crisis for a decade. Migration acted as a safety valve as most of them were migrant sending countries. The departure of a large number of qualified specialists in the 1990s resulted in a brain drain that is still felt in the region today.

Kazakhstan was first to recover among the Central Asian countries around the year 2000 and emerged as an attractive destination for labour migrants from other Central Asian countries. Disparities in economic development and standards of living, as well as geographic closeness and visa free travel (with some exceptions) within the Commonwealth of Independent States (CIS) encouraged workers from neighbouring Central Asian countries, where the supply of labour was excessive and the wages low, to migrate not only to Russia but also to its southern neighbour.

China's growing influence, both cultural and economic, is visible in all Asian countries, including Centra Asia. Recently Nepal has introduced Mandarin in all schools with Chinese funding. Cultural or soft power influence is a long-term and sustainable plan of any project including Belt and Road Initiative (Business Today: 2019). "China's policy of mixing soft diplomacy and economic aid has reaped rich dividends in South Asian countries where India has long held sway, like Sri Lanka and the Maldives" (SCMP: 2018). All these may also lead to more power imbalance in entire Asia with China's influence being the predominant. Central Asia emerging as the new hub of activities with the recent Shanghai Cooperation Organisation (SCO) summit 2019[1] bringing together all major Asian countries in to one umbrella is a new benchmark in the cooperation.

Conclusion

Though India is not a participant country of BRI, yet there will be an impact on it, both politically and economically, as the belt will surround it. India is already dependent on the Chinese manufacturing sector. Any further intensification of industrialisation in this region will definitely influence India's economy. Further, the Chinese political expansionism may not affect India in the short term but it will surely have an impact in the long run as it gets increasingly isolated in the region.

Central Asian regions may benefit from BRI in the short run but they will also risk politically and economically as over dependency on China will undermine their own political sovereignty. Some of the Asian countries such as Vietnam and Cambodia are already feeling suffocated due to China's over domination in the region. This may be a lesson for the countries who have not experienced China's aggressive expansionism.

Given the perpetual conflict in the South Asian and Central Asian region the BRI may either minimise the conflict or maximise it. Only time

1. The SCO was originally rooted in a 1995 treaty, and dubbed the Shanghai Five in 1996, with China, Kazakhstan, Kyrgyzstan, Russia, and Tajikistan as members. Uzbekistan joined in 2001; India and Pakistan joined in 2017. The group was initially focussed on military and border matters between China and what had been the Soviet Union until 1991. Now the SCO transformed into a PAN Asian cooperation in building regional cooperation in a range of issues of peace, economic development and cooperation. https://thediplomat.com/2019/06/the-shanghai-cooperation-organization-summit-kicks-off-in-bishkek/ (accessed 22.06.2019).

will tell as the project evolves. However, the recent Shanghai Cooperation Organization (SCO) summit 2019 in Bishkek, Kyrgyzstan provides fresh hope. Much of the apprehensions in the region are the result of lack of shared vision in the project. However, the conflicting interests and uncertainty can be addressed with the Chinese leadership that provides space for all stakeholders to play a constructive part in the project.

References:

Ahmad, Talmiz Who's Afraid of One Belt One Road? 3 June 2018, The Wire, https://thewire.in/external-affairs/one-belt-one-road-shaping-connectivities-and-politics-in-the-21st-century (accessed 12.04.2018)

Anceschi, L. 2010. Integrating Domestic Politics and Foreign Policy Making: The Cases of Turkmenistan and Uzbekistan. Central Asia Survey 29 (2): 143–158.

Anceschi, Luca. 2015. Turkmenistan's Export Crisis: Is TAPI the Answer? Central Asia Policy Brief 27. http://centralasiaprogram.org/wp-content/uploads/2015/06/Policy-Brief-27-June-2015.pdf. (accessed 01.11. 2016).

Blanchard, Jean-Marc F. and Colin Flint (2017) The Geopolitics of China's Maritime Silk Road Initiative, Geopolitics, 22 (2), 223–245

Brauer, B. 2012. Foreign Direct Investors and National Politics. In Challenges of the Caspian Resource Boom: Domestic Elites and Policy-Making, ed. A. Heinrich and H. Pleines. London: Palgrave Macmillan.

Bunce, V. 1999. The Political Economy of Postsocialism. Slavic Review 58 (4): 756–793.

Businesstoday (2019). Mandarin language compulsory in Nepal schools after China offers to pay teachers' salaries, June 15, https://www.businesstoday.in/latest/trends/mandarin-language-compulsory-in-nepal-schools-after-china-offers-to-pay-teachers-salaries/story/356422.html, (accessed 04.11. 2018).

Chandra, Amiya. 2017. The Trade Game: Engaging with Central Asia, New Delhi: Pentagon Press; Cohen, David. 2008. Global Diaspora, Routledge, New York

Chaudhury, D.R. 2018. Pakistan rejection of China's dam aimed at showing BRI in line with global rules, The Economic Times, https://economictimes.indiatimes.com/news/defence/pakistan-rejection-of-chinas-dam-aimed-at-showing-BRI-in-line-with-global-rules/articleshow/61715963.cms (accessed 03.08.2018)

Choudhury, S. 2012. ONGC Plan to Buy Kazakh Oil Field Stake Is a Sign of Things to Come. Rigzone, November 27. Available from: http://www.rigzone.com/news/oil_gas/a/122379/ONGC_Plan_to_Buy_Kazakh_Oil_Field_Stake_Is_a_Sign_of_Things_to_Come. (accessed 01.11. 2016).

Colucci, Lamont. 2017. Assessing Chinese imperialism: How China will use the One Belt, One Road, September 19, 2017, https://www.washingtontimes.com/news/2017/sep/19/chinese-imperialism-must-be-checked/, (accessed 01.11. 2018).

Cox, R. 1987. Production, Power, and World Order: Social Forces in the Making of History. New York: Columbia University Press.

Epkenhans, Tim. 2016. The Origins of the Civil War in Tajikistan Nationalism, Islamism and Violent Conflict in Post-Soviet Space, Lanham: Lexington Books, https://centralasiaprogram.org/wp-content/uploads/2015/02/Pages-from-Epkenhans-Origins-Tajik-Civil-War-2016-1.pdf (accessed 04.07.2019)

Femia, J.V. 1981. Gramsci's Political Thought: Hegemony, Consciousness and the Revolutionary Process. Oxford: Clarendon Press.

Frankopan, Peter. 2015. The Silk Roads: A New History of the World, London: Bloomsbury

Fuente, Álvaro. 2016. The future of proposed 'new Panama Canal' in doubt, Eueactiv, https://www.euractiv.com/section/development-policy/news/the-future-of-proposed-new-panama-canal-in-doubt/ (accessed 22.04.2018)

Furman, D. 2005. The Regime in Kazakhstan. In Central Asia at the End of the Transition, ed. B. Rumer. Armonk: M.E. Sharpe.

Ghani, Ejaz & Lakshmi Iyer. 2010. Conflict and development, VOX policy portal, https://voxeu.org/article/conflict-and-development-lessons-south-asia (accessed 12.04.2018).

Graham, Lindsay (year not mentioned). A Century of Displacement and Environmental Change, https://www.scribd.com/document/204945344/The-Panama-Canal-A-Century-of-Displacement-and-Environmental-Change (accessed 12.04. 2018).

Hanks, R. 2009. 'Multi-Vector Politics' and Kazakhstan's Emerging Role as a Geo-Strategic Player in Central Asia. Journal of Balkan and Near Eastern Studies 11 (3): 257–267.

Jones Luong, P., and E. Weinthal. 2010. Oil Is Not a Curse: Ownership Structure and Institutions in Soviet Successor States. New York: Cambridge University Press.

Lee, John. 2013. Imaginary lines: the borders of Southeast Asia and the Nusantara, https://openborders.info/blog/imaginary-lines-the-borders-of-southeast-asia-and-the-nusantara/ (accessed 12.07.2018)

Marlene Laruelle. 2018. China's Belt and Road Initiative and its impact in Central Asia, Washington DC: The George Washington University, Central Asia Programme. https://centralasiaprogram.org/wp-content/uploads/2017/12/BRI_Book_.pdf access?

Mazat, N., and F. Serrano. 2013. An Analysis of the Soviet Economic Growth from the 1950's to the collapse of USSR, second draft [Online]. Centro Sraffa. Available from: www.centrosraffa.org/public/bb6ba675-6bef-4182-bb89-339ae1f7e792.pdf. (accessed 12.07.2018)

Morton, A. 2007. Unravelling Gramsci: Hegemony and Passive Revolution in the Global Political Economy. London: Pluto Press.

Naumkin, V. 2006. Uzbekistan's State-Building Fatigue. The Washington Quarterly 29 (3): 127–140.

Nurmakov, A. 2009. Resource Nationalism in Kazakhstan's Petroleum Sector: Curse or Blessing? In Caspian Energy Politics: Azerbaijan, Kazakhstan and Turkmenistan, ed. I. Overland, H. Kjaernet, and A. Kendall Taylor. New York: Routledge.

Nygaard, C. 2012. Regulating Property and Exploitation Rights of Natural Resources. In Challenges of the Caspian Resource Boom: Domestic Elites and Policy-Making, ed. A. Heinrich and H. Pleines. London: Palgrave Macmillan.

Oliker, Olga and Thomas S. Szayna. 2003. Sources of Conflict and Paths to U.S. Involvement, file:///C:/Users/ignou/Downloads/MR1598.pref.pdf, (accessed 04.07.2019)

One Belt, One Road: An Economic Roadmap. 2016. The Economist (Intelligence Unit Report)

Ostrowski, W. 2010. Politics and Oil in Kazakhstan. London: Routledge.

Ostrowski, Wojciech. 2011. Rentierism, Dependency and Sovereignty in Central Asia. In Sovereignty After Empire: Comparing the Middle East and Central Asia, ed. S. Cummings and R. Hinnebusch. Edinburgh: Edinburgh University Press.

Pannier, B. 2015. The Trans-Caspian Pipeline: Technically Possible, Politically Difficult. Radio Free Europe/Radio Liberty. Available from: http://www.rferl.org/a/turkmenistan-natural-gas-europe-pipeline-tcp/27033746.html. (accessed 12.08.2018)

Peyrouse, S. 2007. Economic Aspects of Chinese-Central Asia Rapprochement. Silk Road Paper, Uppsala University.

Pirani, S. 2012. Central Asian and Caspian Gas Production and the Constraints on Export. Oxford Institute for Energy Studies. Available from: https://www.oxfordenergy.org/wpcms/wp-content/uploads/2012/12/NG_69.pdf. (accessed 12.07.2018)

Pomfret, R. 2012. The Economic Future of Central Asia. Brown Journal of World Affairs 19 (1): 59–68.

Sofield, Trevor H.B. 2006. Border Tourism and Border Communities: An Overview, Tourism Geographies, An International Journal of Tourism Space, Place and Environment, 8 (2).

Sorbello, P. 2014. Pipelines and Hegemonies in the Caspian: A Gramscian Appraisal. In Export Pipelines from the CIS Region: National Debates, Political Decision-Making and Geopolitics, ed. A. Heinrich. Stuttgart: Ibidem-Verlag.

Sorbello, P., and L. Grandi. 2013. From Concentration to Competition: The Struggle for Power Between the Kremlin and Gazprom Through the Study of TNK-BP and South Stream. Irish Slavonic Studies 25: 106–119.

Sorbello, Paolo. 2015. The Role of Energy in Russian Foreign Policy Towards Kazakhstan. Energy Brains. http://www.energybrains.org/docs/SL/EnergyBrains_SL_RussiaKazakhstan_PS_2015.pdf (accessed 04.07.2019)

South China Morning Post (SCMP). 2018. China woos Bhutan, at the expense of rival India, https://www.scmp.com/news/china/diplomacy/article/2168951/china-woos-bhutan-expense-rival-india, (accessed 15.03.2019)

Soyres, Francois de, Alen Mulabdic, Siobhan Murray, Nadia Rocha, Michele Ruta. 2018. How the Belt and Road Initiative could reduce trade costs? VOX CEPR Policy Portal, https://voxeu.org/article/how-belt-and-road-initiative-could-reduce-trade-costs (accessed 04.07.2019)

Swanström, Niklas L.P =et al. 2005. A Strategic Conflict Analysis A Strategic Conflict Analysis of Central Asia of Central Asia With a Focus on Kyrgyzstan and Tajikistan, (Prepared for the Swedish Development Cooperation Agency), Central Asia-Caucasus Institute Silk Road Studies Program, https://www.silkroadstudies.org/resources/pdf/Monographs/2005_06_MONO_Swanstrom-Cornell-Tabyshalieva_Conflict-Analysis-Central-Asia.pdf (accessed 04.07.2019)

Syroeshkin, K. 2014. Nuzhno li Kazakhstanu boyat'sya Kitaya: mifi i fobii. Almaty: Institut Mirovoi Ekonomiki i Politiki (IWEP).

The World Economic Forum Report. 2016. Jobs, Jobs, Jobs (presentation by Secretary general world Tourism Organisation), http://reports.weforum.org/travel-and-tourism-competitiveness-report-2017/tourism-and-job-creation-advancing-the-2030-development-agenda/ (accessed 04.07.2019)

World Population Review. 2019. Total Population by Country 2019, http://worldpopulationreview.com/countries/, (accessed 04.07.2019)

Zhukov, S. 2009. Uzbekistan: A Domestically Oriented Gas Producer. In Russian and CIS Gas Markets and Their Impact on Europe, ed. S. Pirani. Oxford: Oxford University Press.

TWO

Prospects, Threats and Challenges of India's 'Connect Central Asia' Policy in the Current International Security Context

Agnieszka Kuszewska

Introduction

The wide-ranging inter-regional cooperation has become a crucial point of reference in the analysis of contemporary international relations and security policy. The states' strategies aimed at economic integration and cooperation with particular regions or particular actors, play significant role in the regional power struggle in the emerging world order. Being an important player, aspiring to enhance its international position, India is putting major effort in expanding its geostrategic role beyond South Asia. 'Connect Central Asia' policy has become one of the major points of reference in India's external policy, but the existing potential for cooperation with Central Asian republics has not been materialised yet. Conspicuously, the India–Central Asia prospects and challenges of connectivity should be subject to a thorough multi-layered academic analysis, with adoption of theoretical and practical approach.

The chapter touches upon the most relevant challenges of India's Central Asia strategy by adhering to the following key assumptions:

- Central Asia plays an enhanced role in the new strategic game engaging powerful Asian players, such as China and India. Their strategies and rivalries will have crucial impact on the security dynamics of the region in the foreseeable future.

- CAR's are geostrategically located at the intersection of Russia, China, Pakistan, Afghanistan and Iran. They are rich in natural resources, with tremendous potential for development; they should be regarded as partners not only as potential goal for the expansion of the spheres of influence by the powerful players.
- India's ambitions as an emerging power with huge energy demands will contribute to enhance its presence in the CAR's and their strategic significance in India's foreign policy will grow.
- India has no direct land connection with Central Asia, but this should not serve as an excuse for expanding and improving the cooperation.

International security context

The rapidly changing security environment pushes the emerging powers to adopt appropriate tactic and introduce continuous and substantial shifts in their international strategies. Willing to enhance their political and economic position, the international actors engage in regional power rivalry. Central Asia, with its exceptional diversities of resources, such as oil, gas, coal, metal ore, has assumed a vital role as a point of reference in the strategies of emerging powers, including India. South and Central Asia are distinctive regions, both playing a noteworthy role in current security complex at the regional and over-regional level. It is therefore crucial to contextualise the significance of both regions within the contemporary security framework, with strong emphasis on the interregional connections and the prospects for enhanced cooperation on multiple levels.

Interregional cooperation and dialogue initiatives are nothing new in international politics (Drechsel 2016: 23). They create multilateral institutional mechanisms to augment economic growth and ensure multi-faceted development. Conspicuously, interregional cooperation became a characteristic feature of contemporary international interactions and a crucial strategic objective of emerging economies, such as India. These strategies are inextricably linked to the South Asian security complex, where India is recognized as the biggest power. Its over-regional strategic capabilities are limited, though. Due to the protracted India-Pakistan conflict South Asia remains war-prone and the least economically integrated region in the world, with weak transport connectivity. New Delhi-Islamabad hostility is deeply marked by profound lack of trust, which further undermines intra-regional economic and political cooperation. Consequently, India faces tremendous security-related challenges and its strategic policy is constructed on the premise of successfully dealing with them. India's foreign policy objectives indicate New Delhi's awareness of a regional security threat coming from Pakistan's fragile domestic political situation along with its limited capability to deal with terrorist problems, and Beijing's expansion (Kuszewska 2015: 225). United States remains engaged in the region, but its global supremacy can no longer be upheld with Chinese hegemonic ambitions, rising Sino-American rivalry and confrontation in Asia. China's increasingly assertive attitude and its 'peaceful rise' evokes concern among India's policymakers. New Delhi therefore seeks a higher position in the international affairs and takes an active part in the promotion of the new world order, based on multipolarity. As Tien-sze Fang (2014: 191–7) points out, India, China and Russia will play significant roles in reshaping a new international order to counterbalance the power of the US. On one hand these three states are engaged in strategic cooperation, on the other they are rivals regarding their influence in the world among developing countries. This power struggle will be visible in Central Asia in the foreseeable future.

India–Central Asia current relations: turning points

Civilisational and cultural relations between India and Central Asia flourished since ancient times due to geographical proximity and geo-cultural affinity. The historically inherited traditions of amicable relations, exchange of people and ideas, as well as goods via many trade routes (Kumar 2007: 9-10), paved the way to develop multi-dimensional linkages.

In the era following the World War II, there are three crucial turning points in India–Central Asia relations. Firstly, the partition of the subcontinent in 1947 and the independence of India, which opened a new chapter in the history of India-CAR's ties. The loss of geographical linkages (due to inception of Pakistan) has limited the chances for strengthening and expanding the cooperation. The Cold War geostrategic situation had direct impact on India's external policy. Although New Delhi wanted to retain its non-aligned position, it gradually developed close ties with the Soviet Union as the major supplier of weaponry and trading partner. Direct Indian-Central Asian interactions were limited during the Cold War, but the context of Indian-Soviet strategic alliance made Delhi relatively present in the lives of the people of Central Asia via television, movies, music, and cultural exchanges (Laruelle, Huchet, Peyrouse, Balci 2010: 2). Secondly, the dissolution of the Soviet Union in 1991, and de jure independence of CAR's, which brought a crucial geopolitical transformation and led to geopolitical emergence of Central Asia as a separate region in the post-Soviet era. When the former Soviet Republics became independent in 1991, India was among the first states which formally recognized them and expressed its will to develop friendly relations. Central Asian Republics have gradually introduced some market-oriented economic reforms to boost economic development and strengthen the competitiveness of private sector. The United States, then the sole superpower, in the mid-1990s enhanced energy-related cooperation by signing an agreement with Kazakhstan to develop the Tengiz oil field. It was followed by a deal inked by the group of energy conglomerates which included BP, Chevron, Exxon Mobil with Azerbaijan in 1994 (Mohapatra 2015: 106). Thirdly, in the first decade of the 21st century, India entered the path of rapid socio-economic development. The emerging power status and ambitions to expand its spheres of interests and provide a secure supply of energy resources, has significantly modified the strategic thinking of India. It was a turning point and new opening for India's Connect Central Asia policy. According to Girijesh Pant (2015:7), 'India's 'Connect Central Asia' policy is premised on comprehensive engagement with the region with energy as its pivot'. Without any doubt, the recent shifts in the global geopolitical realities and the new approach towards Central Asia adopted by powerful actors such as China and United States, became significant in India too. CAR's are no longer perceived as some peripheral areas under strict strategic control of the Soviet Union/ Russia as part of Moscow's direct sphere of influence. On the other hand, Russia as 'traditional hegemon' of the region, has undertaken the policy of regaining its strategic influence there.

'Connect Central Asia' policy: Major prospects, threats, and challenges

Taking into consideration the above mentioned connections between India and Central Asia, the fact that India has undertaken serious initiatives to strengthen relations with ex-Soviet republics should not come as a surprise. It is a natural extension of a historically inherited tradition of multi-faceted cooperation, which laid ground for India's strategic objectives in the region. In the post-Cold War era, India and the Central Asian countries have established bilateral ties in such fields as pharmaceutical sector, textiles, chemicals, hydrocarbons, and metallurgy. Central Asian republics have become one of the largest beneficiaries under the Indian Technical and Economic (ITEC) programme, which was launched in the 1990s. It provided technical assistance and human resource development training to hundreds of specialists from Central Asian states.As an aspiring power, India has redefined its role in international politics and become more assertive. India's economic growth is largely domestic market driven, which makes it relatively resilient, prone to crises (Naidu, Chen 2015: 4). This might be another important factor strengthening India's international economic position. India perceives Central Asia as its 'extended neighbourhood', where it has vital geostrategic interests. The national and international security is interconnected and interdependent as India and Central Asia share unresolved problems and threats such as religious extremism, international terrorism, drug trafficking, etc. The enhanced interaction with CAR's should not be based only on the power struggle agenda by the aspiring, emerging international player (India) materialising its political goals in the strategically important region (Central Asia). The "Connect Central Asia" policy should be clearly delineated as partnership strategy, so the actors engaged could have the sense of historically inherited, equality-based cooperation. Being the largest democracy in the world, India may add special quality to its partnerships and emphasise values-oriented patterns as a crucial element of the institutionalised interconnections between economies, societies and cultures.

Expanding economic relations

India, like other South Asian states, is facing the challenge of boosting its economy to address the persistent multiple socioeconomic problems. On one hand India is aspiring to achieve the more significant position in global leadership with its booming economy and rising middle class, on the other, it has to respond to the challenges of overwhelming poverty, marginalisation and deprivation. One of the fundamental objectives for India's economic growth is to tackle its rapidly growing energy requirements. According to International Energy Agency (2018: 6), India is the third largest energy consumer: 'the United States consumed 16 per cent of world energy, with slightly less than 5 per cent of the world's population. Conversely, China and India consumed 22 per cent and 6 per cent of global energy respectively, but accounted for 20 per cent and 19 per cent of the global population'. Kazakhstan, Uzbekistan and Turkmenistan are rich in hydrocarbon resources, Tajikistan and Kyrgyzstan have a huge potential for the development of hydroelectricity (Shah 2013: 103). It is within India's interest to increase its involvement in the energy sector of Central Asia, and expand cooperation on other issues as the republics of Central Asia are gradually strengthening their geopolitical and economic position in the region.

The initiatives aimed at upgrading the regional cooperation are undertaken by the Central Asian policymakers as they search to expand their presence in the global market of production, services and supplies. In 2006, the then Indian prime minister Manmohan Singh paid official visit to Tashkent and held a meeting with President Islom Karimov. The talks touched upon the issue of exploration acreages to Indian firms in Uzbekistan's energy and mineral sector, including production sharing contracts between ONGC Videsh Limited and Uzbekneftegaz Company. On the eve of the state visit of the President of Uzbekistan Shavkat Mirziyoyev to India (30 September–01 October 2018), the agreement on cooperation between Uzbekneftegaz and ONGC Videsh Limited, a subsidiary of ONGC, the largest state oil and gas corporation of India, was signed. The delegation of Uzbekneftegaz, took part in a business forum with more than 100 representatives of government departments and business circles of Uzbekistan, as well as an exhibition of national products 'Made in Uzbekistan', which were held in New Delhi (UzDaily 2018).

The strategic attitude in Central Asia in the post-Karimov period is shifting in favour of developing an intra-regional cooperation. The first regional summit of Central Asian leaders in Astana, held at Shavkat Mirziyoyev's directive, was aimed at resolving all regional issues, including the Afghanistan imbroglio. India and CAR's are vitally interested in the Afghanistan peace process and successful dealing with the terrorist outfits operating along the Afghanistan-Pakistan border and beyond. The regional diplomatic initiatives aimed at de-escalation of the conflicts might serve as a successful platform for India–Central Asia cooperation. In the second decade of the 21st century, India has undertaken serious initiatives aimed at enhancing the cooperation with CAR's. The first India–Central Asia Dialogue, held on 12-13 June 2012 in Bishkek, was a significant step towards strengthening the ties and building a multi-faceted, longstanding partnership, but the challenges remain overwhelmingly unmet on bilateral and multilateral level.

Kazakhstan, Kyrgyzstan, Tajikistan, Turkmenistan and Uzbekistan have recorded impressive economic growth rates over the last two decades (OECD 2018: 16), but India's trade relations with Central Asia have not reached their potential. The following tables present the latest export and import data regarding India's exchange volume with five Central Asian Republics.[2]

TABLE I India–Kazakhstan export import (in US $ millions) and share in India's total trade

Year	Export	%Share	Import	%Share	Total India-Kazakhstan Trade	%Share	%Growth (Total Trade)
2014–15	250.68	0.08	701.67	0.16	952.35	0.13	3.76
2015–16	151.91	0.06	352.93	0.09	504.84	0.08	-46.99
2016–17	120.88	0.04	521.29	0.14	642.16	0.10	27.20
2017–18	125.37	0.04	907.43	0.19	1,032.81	0.13	60.83

Source: Government of India, Ministry of Commerce and Industry, Department of Commerce: http://commerce-app.gov.in/eidb/

TABLE II India–Kyrgyzstan export/import (in US $ millions) and share in India's global trade

Year	Export	%Share	Import	%Share	Total India-Kyrgyzstan Trade	%Share	%Growth (Total Trade)
2014–15	37.73	0.01	0.77	0.00	38.53	0.01	9.52
2015–16	25.11	0.01	1.79	0.00	26.90	0.00	-30.18
2016–17	30.44	0.01	1.48	0.00	31.93	0.00	18.68
2017–18	28.59	0.01	30.94	0.01	59.53	0.01	86.44

Source: Government of India, Ministry of Commerce and Industry, Department of Commerce: http://commerce-app.gov.in/eidb/

TABLE III India–Tajikistan export/import (in US $ millions) and share in India's global trade

Year	**Export**	%Share	**Import**	%Share	**Total India-Tajikistan Trade**	%Share	**%Growth (Total Trade)**
2014–15	53.71	0.02	4.39	0.00	58.09	0.01	5.38
2015–16	22.26	0.01	9.98	0.00	32.24	0.01	-44.51
2016–17	20.44	0.01	21.82	0.01	42.26	0.01	31.09
2017–18	23.94	0.01	50.29	0.01	74.24	0.01	75.67

Source: Government of India, Ministry of Commerce and Industry, Department of Commerce: http://commerce-app.gov.in/eidb/

TABLE IV India–Turkmenistan export/import (in US $ millions) and share in India's global trade

Year	**Export**	%Share	**Import**	%Share	**Total India-Turkmenistan Trade**	%Share	**%Growth (Total Trade)**
2014–15	91.98	0.03	13.05	0.00	105.03	0.01	19.72
2015–16	68.53	0.03	46.97	0.01	115.50	0.02	9.97
2016–17	57.60	0.02	21.32	0.01	78.92	0.01	-31.67
2017–18	54.31	0.02	26.15	0.01	80.46	0.01	1.95

Source: Government of India, Ministry of Commerce and Industry, Department of Commerce: http://commerce-app.gov.in/eidb/

TABLE V India–Uzbekistan export/import (in US $ millions) and share in India's global trade

Year	Export	%Share	Import	%Share	Total India-Uzbekistan Trade	%Share	%Growth (Total Trade)
2014–15	170.44	0.05	55.86	0.01	226.31	0.03	55.57
2015–16	94.64	0.04	45.23	0.01	139.89	0.02	-38.18
2016–17	108.97	0.04	46.54	0.01	155.51	0.02	11.16
2017–18	132.72	0.04	101.67	0.02	234.39	0.03	50.72

Source: Government of India, Ministry of Commerce and Industry, Department of Commerce: http://commerce-app.gov.in/eidb/

According to the above presented data, the trade relations with Central Asia have declined under the BJP government: the general trend in the India–Central Asia total trade for the years 2015–17 shows a major downfall. In 2018 the situation started to improve gradually, for example with the over 50 per cent growth in India's total trade with Uzbekistan. There is a huge decline in India's export to Kazakhstan and gradual surge in import from Kazakhstan since Narendra Modi came to power.

Kazakhstan is the most important trading partner of India with a turnover of $1,032.81 billion and Uzbekistan is the second, with turnover paltry $234.39 million. Unfortunately, their share in India's total import/export remains quite insignificant. Altogether, the trade relations with Central Asia remain just at 0.19 per cent of India's overall foreign exchange (0.11% of India's overall export, 0.24% of India's import). There is much to be done to expand these relations.

In 2017–18 the total value of India's exports to all five Central Asian republics was a paltry $364.93 million, largely dominated by the pharmaceutical products ($132.77 million); India is one of the major exporters of pharmaceutical products to Central Asia. Indian tea remains popular in Central Asian states, but it has to compete with Sri Lankan and Kenyan. To compare, India's total commodity export to the USA in the same budget year reached $47,878.16 billion, and to China touched $13,333.53 billion.

TABLE VI. Export. Top 3 commodities exported from India to CAR's in 2017–18 and their values (in US$ Million)

Country	Commodity and value in US$ Million
Kazakhstan (total export in 2017–18: 125.37)	1. Pharmaceutical products: 38.35 2. Coffee, tea, mate and spices: 27.58 3. Nuclear reactors, boilers, machinery and mechanical appliances; parts thereof: 13.26
Kyrgyzstan (total export in 2017–18: 28.59)	1. Articles of apparel and clothing accessories, knitted and not knitted or crocheted: 14.19 2. Pharmaceutical products: 8.02 3. Articles of leather, saddlery and harness, travel goods, handbags: 1.41
Tajikistan (total export in 2017–18: 23.94)	1. Pharmaceutical products: 18.43 2. Meat and edible meat offal: 1.69 3. Coffee, tea, mate and spices: 1.22
Turkmenistan (total export in 2017–18: 54.31)	1. Meat and edible meat offal: 27.85 2. Pharmaceutical products: 15.20 3. Nuclear reactors, boilers, machinery and mechanical appliances; parts thereof: 3.48
Uzbekistan (total export in 2017–18: 132.72)	1. Pharmaceutical products: 52.77 2. Nuclear reactors, boilers, machinery and mechanical appliances; parts thereof: 35.17 3. Coffee, tea, mate and spices: 3.83

Source: Government of India, Ministry of Commerce and Industry, Department of Commerce: http://commerce-app.gov.in/eidb/

In 2017–18 the total value of India's imports from all five Central Asian republics stood at $1,116.48 billion and was largely dominated by mineral fuels and oils and products of their distillation ($768.05 million) imported mostly from Kazakhstan. To compare, India's total commodity import from the USA reached $26,611.03 billion, and from China touched $76,380.70 billion.

TAB. VI. Import. Top 3 commodities imported to India from CAR's in 2017–18 and their values (in US$ Million)

Country	Commodity and value in US$ Million
Kazakhstan (total import in 2017–18: 907.43)	1. Mineral fuels, mineral oils and products of their distillation; bituminous substances; mineral waxes: 738.10 2. Ores, slag and ash: 79.59 3. Salt; sulphur; earths and stone; plastering materials, lime and cement: 26.08
Kyrgyzstan (total import in 2017–18: 30.94)	1. Mineral fuels, mineral oils and products of their distillation; bituminous substances; mineral waxes: 29.95 2. Edible vegetables and certain roots and tubers: 0.60 3. Edible fruit and nuts: 0.06
Tajikistan (total import in 2017–18: 50.29)	1. Aluminium and articles thereof: 37.98 2. Ores, slag and ash: 10.97 3. Cotton: 0.95
Turkmenistan (total import in 2017–18: 26.15)	1. Inorganic chemicals: 12.25 2. Cotton: 5.94 3. Salt; sulphur; earths and stone; plastering materials, lime and cement: 4.13
Uzbekistan (total import in 2017–18: 101.67)	1. Natural or cultured pearls; precious or semiprecious stones; pre. metals; imit. jewellery: 64.25 2. Edible vegetables and certain roots and tubers: 11.83 3. Fertilizers: 8.93

Source: Government of India, Ministry of Commerce and Industry, Department of Commerce: http://commerce-app.gov.in/eidb/

Both India's export and import of commodities to/from Central Asian republics remain at a very low level, and the existing potential should be enhanced in the upcoming years. It is within the interest of both India and the Central Asian republics. There is an urgent need to reconsider India's Central Asia policy and this will be a crucial geostrategic challenge for the new Indian government which will come to power as a result of the parliamentary elections scheduled for April 2019. The overall potential benefits for India and CAR's in pursuing the trade relations and other 'Connect Central Asia' objectives are multifaceted:

- Greater connectivity with India's 'extended neighbourhood'.
- Reconstruction of old historical Silk Route connections and create new transit/trade corridors.
- Enhanced competitiveness of landlocked Central Asian states and access to the new markets.
- Support for development of knowledge technology in Central Asia.
- Development of peace, security and regional stability.
- Boosted cooperation on countering terrorism and fundamentalism.
- Addressing huge energy needs of India's developing economy.
- Diversification of energy sources for India.

Regional security factor

The relations between India and Central Asian Republics and the prospects for strengthening the ties have to be analysed in the broader context of regional security complex. Such important international actors as China and Russia must be taken into consideration while discussing the new power game in the region. India is concerned about the revival of Islamic radicalism in Central Asia and the connection with the region is blocked by the two politically unstable countries: Afghanistan and Pakistan. This factor along with the rivalry with China, remains crucial in assessing India's capabilities of expanding its strategic and socio-economic connectivity initiatives in the region of Central Asia.

China has a long tradition of relations with Central Asia, dating back to the ancient Silk Road. In the second decade of the 21st century Chinese diplomacy enhanced its activity in Central Asia, challenging the Russia's domination. China has a crucial advantage over India regarding the direct connectivity with CAR's. It shares borders with three Central Asian republics: Kazakhstan, Kyrgyzstan, and Tajikistan. Beijing remains apprehensive about its Western border and stability in Xinjiang province inhabited by a significant (approx. 46%) Muslim minority. China has also invested in building roads and railways to deliver its goods to the region and is engaged in energy projects with Uzbekistan and Kazakhstan (Zhu 2010: 112). Lacking direct connection India has limited prospects for containing China's expansion in Central Asia. There is increased uncertainty as to how this rivalry will unfold and how it will shape the regional security landscape in the upcoming decades. India, along with Pakistan, became a full member of the Shanghai Cooperation Organization (SCO) at the Astana Summit held on June 8–9, 2017. It is a political platform which includes Russia, China, Pakistan and Central Asia. Taking into consideration the India–Pakistan conflict and other rivalries within the organization, there is a limited chance that SCO will play a significant role as a tool for de-escalation of existing tensions.

Any analysis on the India–Central Asia connectivity is incomplete without taking on board the threats and challenges arising out of the situation in Pakistan and Afghanistan.

Since the partition of the Subcontinent, India and Pakistan, the two major South Asian states, have been engaged in the unresolved conflict in Kashmir. Their relations are prone to escalation and marked by huge trust deficit. The early 2019 saw the sharp escalation of bilateral relations in the aftermath of the suicide terrorist attack in India-administered Kashmir, where over 40 members of security personnel were killed. India, accusing Pakistan on supporting Islamic radical outfits, declared it will ensure the 'complete isolation' of Pakistan (BBC News: 2019). This escalation-prone conflict and lack of cooperation in South Asia has an impact on limited prospects for expanding the cooperation with Central Asia by India. Permanent rivalry between New Delhi and Islamabad weakens both states and their position as regional players. As Laumullin (2006: 29) emphasised, "'While India and Pakistan fight each other for the expansion of their prospective influence in Central Asia, other states gain actual economic and political power in the region".

Due to its geographical location, Afghanistan is perceived as a crucial linkage between South and Central Asia and successful peace initiatives are crucial for India as it enhances the connectivity via Chabahar port. The protracted unrest in Afghanistan and the activities of jihadi outfits remain a serious threat to the peace and security of Central Asia and South Asia (Dhaka 2005: 135) and a crucial impediment for the regional stabilisation. The Trump administration's efforts aimed at engaging the Taliban into the peace talks, signify the failure of American 17-year long 'war on terror' campaign in Afghanistan and pose a threat that the solution of the conflict will be tantamount to the continuous presence of religious extremists in political power. The situation in Afghanistan and the reconstruction of this country will be a major point of reference in India's regional strategy. New Delhi has been engaged in the infrastructure projects and reconstruction of Afghanistan, developing strategic partnership with Kabul. Last decade brought a shift from traditional perception of Afghanistan as the territory of rivalry with Pakistan, to the strategic perception as the source of minerals and the gateway to Central Asian energy and markets to fulfil India's industrialisation needs.

The problem of connectivity remains a crucial challenge for the future, but it is a problem which can be successfully dealt with by expanding the cooperation with Iran, which is the perfect transit country for India and may serve as the gateway to Central Asia and Russia (Stobdan 2017). The trilateral transit agreement was signed by India, Iran and Afghanistan in Tehran in May 2016. It was announced in December 2018, that the agreement will be officially implemented in early spring of 2019. It allows transit of Indian goods to Afghanistan via Iran's south-eastern port of Chabahar, bypassing Pakistan. It links ports in the western coast of India to the strategically important Chabahar port and covers the road and rail links between Chabahar and the Afghan border. Tashkent could join the agreement as Chabahar port becomes the nearest sea port for Uzbekistan and could act as a real 'game changer' if the trade corridors could include Central Asia (Stobhan 2017). Being landlocked is a huge strategic disadvantage and challenge for Central Asian republics as it requires enhanced economic cooperation and integration with other states. The access to sea ports such as Chabahar and construction of railways could expand Central Asia's cooperation with India, Afghanistan and Iran. The transit routes for oil and gas exports will strengthen the economic position of Central Asia and limit the Russia's strategic domination. India has also invested in the International North South Transport Corridor (INSTC).

Conclusion

India's 'Connect Central Asia' policy faces many challenges and threats, but at the same time it has enormous potential to reconstruct the historical connections and open the new ones. Central Asian states hold tremendous importance to India as its neighbourhood and it a significant challenge to create more effective and full-fledged interactions with them. The major problem is how to use the existing opportunities and address all the issues properly without unceasingly referring to the impediments of physical connectivity. The dynamically changing geostrategic realities call for the formulation of the new narratives regarding India's Central Asia strategy. The advantages on India's side are tremendous: its long-lasting historical ties, common cultural traditions, the experiences based on good relations create a natural background for an enhanced cooperation. The strategic, decisive shift to a strategic, mutually beneficial partnership should be introduced.

The recent developments give clear indications that Central Asian Republics play a crucial role in India's emerging regional aspirations. India's future policy towards Central Asia will be based on the strategic significance of CAR's to India's geopolitical interests regarding the New Delhi's quest for 'strategic depth' in its 'extended neighbourhood'. India's rising need for energy resources and potentially mutually beneficial trade cooperation along with facing other challenges such as terrorism and extremism in the Central and South Asia, should count as crucial factors motivating the decision makers on both sides. It will require enormous diplomatic and political skills to enhance India's engagement in the region, which China and Russia consider their sphere of influence. The inclusion of India as a full member of Shanghai Cooperation Organization in 2017 brought new opportunities and channels for the interactions with the CAR's, but on the other hand the presence of Pakistan in the organization may bring their bilateral conflict and protracted conflict to the forum of SCO.

Lack of direct connections with Central Asia, protracted conflict and unchangeably hostile relations with Pakistan, instability in Afghanistan remain the most significant obstacles for developing the relations, but it should not be used as an excuse for developing ties with CAR. There is no doubt that peace in the Indian subcontinent is one of the major obstacles to the regional development. Taking into consideration the conflict-prone relations between India and Pakistan, the chances for the permanent solution of this bilateral rivalry are largely limited in the foreseeable future. India's 'Connect Central Asia' policy will have to take this fact into consideration. While enhancing the cooperation with Central Asia, the architects of India's foreign and security policy should realise that it is crucial to think beyond the economic prism and take into consideration the larger socio-political and cultural context. If this challenge is appropriately addressed, the new initiatives can create more opportunities for the successful development of cross-regional linkages. Rich national resources guarantee enormous potential for further development, enhanced cooperation on multiple levels, which will be beneficial for both sides. Apart from the need for boosting the trade relations, there are plenty of issues of common concern which India and CAR's share, such as radicalism, terrorism, separatism, drug trafficking. This cooperation should be based on people-oriented approach with special reference to the regional socio-cultural realities. India's strategic thinking should be based on the geopolitical objectives aimed at creation of more conducive environment for advancing these goals. There are many potentially successful initiatives, which may open the gates to the Central Asian markets, such as investments in the Iranian port of Chabahar or the International North South Transport Corridor. From the perspective of a Central European researcher, whose country strongly benefitted from regional integration within the European Union, the best way to prosperity is multi-faceted, enhanced cooperation. The major question which should be dealt with comes down to how to overcome the existing problems, what elements of cooperation can be introduced in the current geopolitical reality, what strategic decisions should be made within the next few years.

The Indian decision makers should thoroughly define India's priorities and interests for the upcoming years and design the appropriate strategy towards Central Asian republics. They should discuss with their Central Asian partners how to effectively tackle the security-related obstacles and implement the cooperation initiatives in particular areas. Emphasis should be put on enhanced direct people-to-people contacts on bilateral and multilateral level, for example academic conferences, business seminars, cultural programmes, students/experts exchange initiatives, establishment of chambers of commerce with experts and business community from India and particular Central Asian states.

References

Djaka, A. (2005) South Asia and Central Asia: Geopolitical Dynamics. Jaipur: Mangal Deep Publications.

Drechsel, B. (2016) Interregionale Beziehungen und strategische Partnerschaften. Die EU, Indien und Brasilien in der internationalen Politik. Wiesbaden: Springer VS.

Fang, T. (2014) Asymmetrical Threat Perceptions in India–China Relations. New Delhi: Oxford University Press.

Government of India, Ministry of Commerce and Industry, Department of Commerce, Export-Import Data Bank, Country-wise. Retrieved from: http://commerce-app.gov.in/eidb/ (14.02.2019).

International Energy Agency (2018) World Energy Balances: Overview. Retrieved from: https://webstore.iea.org/world-energy-balances-2018-overview (21.02.2018).

Kumar, B. B. (2007) 'India and Central Asia. Links and Interactions' (pp. 3–33), in: Roy, J. N.; Kumar, B.B. (eds.) India and Central Asia. Classical to Contemporary Periods. New Delhi: Concept Publishing Company.

Kuszewska, A. (2015) 'Central Europe, the European Union and Asia', in: F. Erixon, K. Srinivasan (eds.), Europe in Emerging Asia. Opportunities and Obstacles in Political and Economic Encounters (pp. 209–32). London-New York: Rowman & Littlefield.

Laruelle, M.; Huchet, J-F., Peyrouse, S.; Balci, B. (2010) 'Why Central Asia? The Strategic Rationale of Indian and Chinese Involvement in the Region' (pp. 1–8), in: Laruelle, M.; Huchet, J-F., Peyrouse, S.; Balci, B (eds.) China and India in Central Asia A New "Great Game"? New York: Palgrave Macmillan.

Laumullin, M. (2006) 'The Contemporary Geopolitical Situation in Central Asia and India's Interests, in: Santhanam, K.; Sultanov, B. K. (eds.) India–Kazakhstan Relations: Enhancing the Partnership. New Delhi: Anamaya Publishers.

Mohapatra, N. K. (2015) 'Geopolitics of Energy Security in Central Asia: Implications for India'(pp. 37–46), in: Pant, G. (ed.) India's Emerging Energy Relations. New Delhi: Springer India.

Naidu, G.V.C.; Chen, M. (2015) 'Introduction' (pp. 1–8), in: Naidu, G.V.C.; Chen, M.; Narayanan, R. (eds.) India and China in the Emerging Dynamics of East Asia. New Delhi–Heidelberg-New York–Dordrecht–London: Springer.

OECD (2018) Competitiveness and Private Sector Development. Enhancing Competitiveness. in Central Asia. Retrieved from: https://doi.org/10.1787/20765762 (04.02.2019).

Pant. G. (2015) 'Introduction. India's Emerging Energy Relations: Issues and Challenges' (pp. 1–16), in: Pant. G. (ed.) India's emerging Energy Relations. Issues and Challenges. New Delhi: Springer.

Shash, M. S. (2013) 'Energy Cooperation between Central Asia and South Asia: Prospects and Challenges' (pp. 101–18), in: Malhotra, R.; Gill, S. S.; Gaur, N. (eds.) Perspectives on Bilateral and Regional Cooperation. South and Central Asia. Centre for Rural and Industrial Development: Chandigarh.

Stobdan, P. (2017) To Make Chabahar a 'Game Changer' Central Asian States Need to Be Roped In. Institute for Defence Studies and Analyses (IDSA). Retrieved from: https://idsa.in/idsacomments/to-make-chabahar-a-game-changer-central-asian-states_pstobdan_121217 (24.02.2018).

UzbekDaily (2018) 'Uzbek Uzbekneftegaz and ONGC Videsh Limited Sign Cooperation Agreement'. UzDaily, 09. October 2018, Retrieved from: https://www.uzdaily.com/articles-id-46067.htm (25.02.2018).

Zhu, Z. (2010) China's New Diplomacy. Rationale, Strategies and Significance. Burlington: Ashgate Publishing Limited.

THREE

India's Connectivity Push and Road to Central Asia

Poonam Mann

The study of the terrestrial dimensions of international politics has acquired a lot of interest among the political scientists, strategists and journalists in the past few years. Through their scholarly work, they have tried to revive the importance and influence of geographical factors while studying international relations. Although the history of geopolitical speculation dates back to the times of Kautilya and Aristotle, however, distinctive geopolitical thinking did not develop until the second half of 19th and first half of 20th century when a number of theorists ,like Halford Mackinder, Alferd Mahan, Friedrich Ratzel, E.C.Semple, Huntington, Rudolf Kjellen, etc., heavily emphasised on the role of geographical factors/geopolitics in international relations, through their writings. (Bandyopadhyaya, 1979) Seemingly, they tried to abet "geography's 'revenge' against the perceptions of obsolescence in the face of changing technology", modernisation and economic development (Fettweis, 2015: 233).

Robert D. Kaplan's work in signifying the influence of geography upon great power politics in The Revenge of Geography – What the Map Tells Us About Coming Conflicts and The Battle Against Fate, is a point in case where he argues that, "The world is certainly not flat and that the first step in understanding great power politics of 21st century is still to look at a map" (Ikenberry, 2012). Moreover, while emphasising the influence of geography on geopolitics, he states that, "Geopolitics is the battle of – is the struggle for space and power and how often the nations that are next to each other can be enemies while a nation far away can be a friend balancing against the enemy" (Kaplan, 2012). Therefore, it can be gathered that geography is the most fundamental factor in shaping the foreign policy of a country as it is the most permanent.

Against this background, India–Central Asia relations hold their own importance. The relationship which is centuries old due to historical, cultural, civilisational and ethnic ties has not been able to achieve its full potential, and geography has remained one of the important impediments. In this context, two points are worth-mentioning: One, to understand Central Asia as the 'Heartland' of international affairs and two, lack of geographical proximity between India and the Central Asian region.

Central Asia as the 'Heartland'

The British geographer, Sir Halford J. Mackinder in his "Heartland Theory" and Dutch-born American scholar Nicolas J. Spykman's work gave a fair amount of analysis about how the Central Asian Republics (CARs) attracted the attention of various global and regional powers immediately after their independence due to their geostrategic location. Mackinder in his three essays, "The geographical Pivot of History" (1904), "Democratic Ideals and Reality" (1919), and "The Round World and the Winning of the Peace" (1945) further expanded and refined his ideas on geopolitics that how it has conditioned the behaviour of the states throughout history including his famous "Heartland Theory" (Sempa, 2015: 613). He perceived that Central Asia's geography made it the world's most important place, labelling it as the "pivot region of the world's politics" and the "Heartland." He went on to assert that command of this "Heartland" inevitably leads to command of the entire world. In his words: "Who rules East Europe commands the Heartland: Who rules the Heartland commands the World-Island: Who rules the World-island commands the World" (Fettweis, 2000: 58). Besides, expanded Central Asia formulates the 'geo-political pivot' of Eurasia, that covers around 40 per cent of the earth's surface, sheltering almost 70 per cent of global population (4.9. billion people) and producing 60-65 per cent of the world GDP (Kang and Won, 2016). It, thus, holds a major part of the global demographic, geographical and economic potential along with richness of natural resources. Consequently, offering enormous appeal to various global and regional players. In the past few years, an unprecedented interest of various players has been witnessed in Eurasia. The belief is that multiple advantages could be gained by engaging with this somewhat open-ended global space. As Zbigniew Brzezinski illustrated 'Eurasia to be the chessboard for future fights among world's leading states…and that struggle involves geostrategy' (Brzezinski, 1997).

Besides geostrategy, the Central Asian region also offers a variety of economic opportunities to the global/regional powers that include favourable terms of trade and effective transit routes (Sanghera and Satybaldieva, 2018). The region represents the ancient 'silk road' that had facilitated business and cultural exchanges between Europe and Asia in the past. These routes are now being revived as 'New Silk Road' and a number of initiatives to transit through the region have been floated. Prominent among these are China-led Belt and Road Initiative (BRI), Russian vision of Eurasian Economic Union (EEU) and the United States' longstanding vision of connecting South and Central Asia under New Silk Roads project. Each of them is trying to shape the region as per their own vision and strategies, and hence striving for different outcomes (Sanghera and Satybaldieva, 2018), thus also creating a competitive environment and resultant connectivity complexities. For instance, China is promoting various developmental projects in these republics in order to connect it with its underdeveloped and restive province of Xinjiang; Russian attempts to integrate them in its new regional organisations are aimed at keeping these republics away from the West and the US attempts to create connections between Central Asia and South Asia or with Europe are aimed to bypass Russia. On the other hand, the CARs are increasingly looking towards these powers for their investment in infrastructural projects in the region and to gain access to international markets. Such opportunities will help them to get out of their land-locked position to being land-linked to the world's great and dynamic economies (Linn, 2012). Against the backdrop of such complexities India has to navigate and make its own space within the region.

Geographical proximity between India and CAR's

Orthodoxly, India has been regarded as a major power in the South Asian region, however, due to the country's geo-strategic location, Central Asia, West Asia and the Indo-Pacific region span within its security and economic interests which resemble an expanded geopolitical theatre. These strategic neighbourhoods hold prominence in the post-cold war context of emerging threats and opportunities in various sectors such as energy security, terrorism, search for new markets and investment opportunities, etc., for Indian entrepreneurs.

However, the focus of this paper is limited to the geopolitics of India's extended neighbourhood—Central Asia, where, post-partition geography and Great Himalayan barrier have made it hard for India to develop geographical connectivity with the region. The absence of direct physical access has been a major stumbling block in India's relations with Central Asia. Tajikistan is the nearest Central Asian country for India which shares its borders with Afghanistan. A narrow strip of Wakhan Corridor in Afghanistan separates India from Tajikistan. But the geographical proximity of this corridor to Pakistani-administered Kashmir, compels the strategists and scholars to look at the region from a different perspective. Besides, geo-strategic rivalry with China further ensured that connectivity through the Himalayan region remain inaccessible. Hence, tough geopolitical neighbourhood has dissuaded India's reach into the region. Consequently, with no direct road transportation access, India's trade and commercial relations with CARs remained miniscule. India's trade volume with all the five Central Asian republics has remained less than USD 1 billion. In an attempt to redeem the situation, India has to seek new avenues for its outreach to the Central Asian region either through regional and multilateral engagements or close cooperation with friendly countries like Russia, Iran and Afghanistan, around the region.

Iran as a facilitator in India–Central Asia Cooperation

"Iran occupies a pivotal position on the tripolar chessboard. Geographically, it is the only nation that abuts both the Persian Gulf and the Caspian Sea, positioning itself to play a significant role in two areas of greatest energy concern. Further, Iran abuts the Strait of Hormuz—the narrow waterway from the Persian Gulf to the Indian Ocean through which about one quarter of the world's oil moves every day. If Washington ever lifts its trade embargo on Iran, its territory could be used as the most obvious transit route for the delivery of oil and gas from the Caspian countries to global markets. Moreover, Iran possesses the world's second largest reserves of petroleum and also the second largest reserves of natural gas. Though Iran possess less oil than the Saudis and lesser gas than the Russians, it is certain that no other country controls so much of both these vital energy resources" (Klare and Engelhardt, 2006: 57). It may be noted that while addressing the Central Asian leaders, the then President of Iran, Mr. Rafsanjani, mentioned that, "Cooperation should certainly be carried out via Iran. For links between the north to the south, the east and the west, these countries and Europe, Europe and Asia, everything should cross Iran – oil and gas pipelines, railways, communication routes and international airports" (Menashri, 1998: 57).

Hence, there is no ambiguity that the centrality of Iran in terms of its geographical location is vital. But the trade embargo on Iran in recent years is recognised as a factor that nullifies its privileged position on the global energy map (Menashri, 1998: 57). While taking the above-mentioned quotes into account, clearly, India's current coöperation with Iran is primarily centred around its energy security and access to Central Asian region and Afghanistan, holds merit. Also, Iran can help in fulfilling India's desire to reclaim the influence and cultural relations it uses to enjoy with the CARs before the dawn of colonialism.

Currently, India–Iran relations are being seen through the prism of acceleration in the development of the strategic Chabahar Port. Undoubtedly, the development of the Port in the Gulf of Oman is a key project between the two countries, because it gives India the access to Afghanistan and CARs, bypassing Pakistan on the one hand and helping Iran to become a transit route to CARs and Afghanistan and reintegrating itself with the global economy on the other hand. Besides, if everything goes right, the project will give Afghanistan an easy access to the markets of CARs, West Asia and Europe, and thus will help in integrating Afghan economy with the region as well as the world. Similarly, the CARs will also be able to access Indian and Afghan markets. It will be a positive outcome for all parties involved.

The role of Chabahar

Chabahar Port is located in the Sistan-Baluchistan province on the south-eastern coast of Iran. As mentioned earlier, its significance lies in the fact that the port will give India sea-land access into Afghanistan and through Iran's eastern borders, to Central Asian region. The discussions to develop the Chabahar port complex between India and Iran started in 2003 (Press information bureau, 2019), but finally the deal was materialised in 2016. During Indian Prime Minister, Narendra Modi's visit to Iran in May 2016, a commercial contract for the development and operations of Chabahar Port was signed between Indian Joint Venture India Ports Global Pvt Ltd (a Consortium of Jawaharlal Nehru Port Trust and Kandla Port Trust) and Iran's Arya Banader. The bilateral agreement provided India the right to develop and operate two terminals and five berths with multipurpose cargo handling capacities in the port of Chabahar for ten years (Press Information Bureau, 2019). At the same time a Trilateral Transport and Transit Corridor agreement was signed between India, Iran and Afghanistan for connecting Chabahar with the Afghan road and rail network.

As mentioned above, Chabahar has two terminals—Shahid Kalantari and Shahid Beheshti. Shahid Kalantari is handling about 2.1 million tonnes of cargo per year and with the operationalisation of Shahid Beheshti, the capacity is expected to go up to 10 million tonnes (Stobdan, 2017). The first phase of the Shahid Beheshti was completed in December 2017 and the first shipment of 1.1 million tonnes of wheat through Chabahar Port to Afghanistan proved that it could become a reliable alternative for India's access to Central Asian region as well (Bhattacherjee, 2017). This connectivity can be strengthened through bilateral or multilateral initiatives. So far, India has completed the 218-kilometer road from Delaram (Afghanistan) to Zaranj on the Afghanistan-Iran border. Further, India's assistance for building Chabahar-Zahedan Railway was discussed, during Iranian President Hassan Rouhani's visit to India in February 2018, so that full potential of port could be realized to connect it to Afghanistan and Central Asia (Indian Express, 2018). Besides, India, as it does not have any direct connectivity with the Central Asian region, is trying to create a link. An important step in this direction is India's accession to Ashgabat Agreement (Ministry of External Affairs, Government of

India, 2018). Ashgabat Agreement is a transit pact established in 2011 by Iran, Oman, Qatar, Uzbekistan and Turkmenistan to develop trade and transport with Iranian and Omani ports (The Hindu, 2015). The land component of the agreement includes rail links through Kazakhstan-Uzbekistan-Turkmenistan and Iran. However, Qatar had withdrawn from the agreement in 2013 and Kazakhstan has joined it. Accession to the agreement would enable India to utilise this existing transport and transit corridor to facilitate trade and commercial interaction with the Eurasian region (Press Information Bureau, 2016) and would synchronise India's efforts to implement International North South Transport Corridor (INSTC) for enhanced connectivity.

The INSTC—considered as India's gateway to expand trade and investment links with Central Asian republics and Eurasia—is a multi-modal transportation route that links the Indian Ocean and Persian Gulf to the Caspian Sea via Iran and onwards to northern Europe via St. Petersburg in Russia. It envisages movement of goods from Mumbai (India) to Bandar Abbas (Iran) by sea, from Bandar Abbas to Bandar-e Anzali (an Iranian port on the Caspian Sea) by road and then from Bandar-e-Anzali to Astrakhan (a Caspian Port in the Russian Federation) by ship across the Caspian Sea, and thereafter from Astrakhan to the other regions of the Russian Federation and further into Europe by Russian railways. The INSTC project was initiated by Russia, Iran and India in September 2000, in order to establish transportation network among the member states and enhance connectivity with land-locked CARs. Later, it was joined by another eleven countries, namely: Armenia, Azerbaijan, Kazakhstan, Kyrgyz Republic, Tajikistan, Turkey, Ukraine, Belarus, Oman, Syria and Bulgaria is an observer member (Sharma and Menezes, 2018). The progress on this project, however, has been very slow in the past. But, in 2014, in order to understand the problem areas and to realise the full potential of the corridor, a dry run was conducted by the Federation of Freight Forwarder's Association in India (FFFAI), on the NhavaSheva-Bandar Abbas (Iran) - Baku (Azerbaijan) and the NhavaSheva - Badar Abbas - Amirabad (Iran) - Astrakhan (Russia) route via Caspian Sea. The dry run report pointed out that, "The proposed INSTC route via Bandar Abbas in Iran to Russia and CIS (Commonwealth of Independence States) destinations in transit through Iran could be the best route with optimal transit/cost for the Indian exporters/importers (Press Information Bureau, 2014). Further, in 2015, the officials from India, Iran, Russia and other eleven countries had a meeting in New Delhi and approved draft transit and customs agreements for INSTC. This will provide the legal framework for moving freight on ship-rail-road route linking India, Iran, Russia, CARs and Europe (Choudhary, 2015).

To operationalise this project, India is making attempts to fill in the missing links with cooperation from CARs. During the Indian PM's visit to Kazakhstan in July 2015, India agreed on increased collaboration in the framework of International North South Transport Corridor (INSTC) and agreed that Kazakhstan–Turkmenistan–Iran (KTI) rail link, which was operationalised in December 2014, should become a linked corridor of the INSTC (Ministry of External Affairs, Government of India, 2015). The route links the Caspian Sea to the Indian Ocean through the Bandar Abbas and Chabahar ports in Iran. Also, Kazakhstan's national railway company, Kazakhstan TemirZholy (KTZ) signed a Memorandum of Understanding with SEZ Adnani Ports for building a port in Mundra (Gujarat). The importance of this port lies in the fact that once the link with Mundra Port and Bandar Abbas is ready, the goods can be transported via KTI rail link and this will be shorter and cheaper (The Statesman, 2015).

Moreover, India's potential participation in Eurasian Economic Union (EEU) would be an additional advantage. India and EEU (comprising Belarus, Kyrgyzstan, Kazakhstan, Russia, and Armenia) are currently studying the feasibility of a Free Trade Agreement (FTA). Undoubtedly, an FTA with EEU would bring benefits for Indian economy. It will not only help in boosting India's trade with Eurasian countries but also help in improving connectivity (Sekhani, 2015).

Thus, India-Iran involvement in all these connectivity projects along with Chabahar Port facilitates India's outreach to its extended neighbourhood. Once fully operational, all these projects will be instrumental in increasing the trade and commerce with this region.

Afghanistan as a Facilitator in India–Central Asia Relations

While discussing Iran's importance in India–Central Asia relations in the previous section, importance of Afghanistan as a possible transit country to Central Asia is well understood and also how through various transport connectivity projects, India's reach to Afghanistan and CARs has become possible. Here, one factor demands due attention that Uzbekistan played a very important role in getting India into Ashgabat agreement that would complement India's maritime link with Oman via the Duqm port (Choudhary, 2018). Further, Uzbekistan is contributing by building a rail-road from Termez on Uzbek-Afghan border to Mazar-e-Sharif in Afghanistan that will be further extended to Sheberghan, Maymana and then Herat and from here, the doubly land-locked Uzbekistan will be one step closer to the sea—i.e. Chabahar Port via Afghan-Iranian rail projects (Putz, 2017). These rail-road construction projects in Afghanistan, undertaken by Uzbekistan compliments India's participation in the Chabahar Port project. Such convergence of interest will surely help in strengthening India-Uzbek relations. Thus, Afghanistan as a transit point will help in facilitating India's relations with CARs.

Secondly, Afghanistan also acts as a crucial link between South Asia and Central Asia for enhancing energy and economic cooperation. Turkmenistan-Afghanistan-Pakistan-India (TAPI) gas pipeline is an appropriate example in this context. Rich in Hydrocarbon resources, the CARs are looking for diverse markets and Hydrocarbon Scarce South Asian countries (above mentioned) complement each other in this endeavour. The TAPI gas pipeline project offers beneficial results to all four participating countries. Once completed, the project may go a long way in diversifying Turkmenistan's quest for exporting vast gas exports; it would generate revenue and allow diversification of export routes. For India and Pakistan, it would address energy deficits and in Afghanistan, it would provide revenue for development and gas for industrial enterprises.

TAPI has come a long way after its initial conceptualisation in 1995, promoted by the US The project was put on the back burner in 1998, owing to fighting in Taliban controlled Afghanistan and later the US and ISAF operations in Afghanistan following 9/11 attacks (Bohr, 2016). At the end of the Taliban regime, the project was revived and Afghanistan – Pakistan–Turkmenistan signed a new agreement at the end of 2002. The Asian Development Bank (ADB) conducted a feasibility study of the project and gave its consent to sponsor the project in 2005. In April 2008, India joined the three countries and finally in December 2010, after nearly two years of intergovernmental deliberations, the Presidents of Turkmenistan, Afghanistan and Pakistan and India's Energy Minister signed a framework agreement at a summit in Ashgabat to build the 1,800-kilometre (km) pipeline (Rad, 2012: 83-84).

The 1,800-km long pipeline, of which 200 km will run through Turkmenistan, 773 km- Afghanistan, 827 km- Pakistan to Fazilka in India, will be built at the estimated cost of $10 billion. TAPI will carry gas from Turkmenistan's Galkynysh field (also known as South Yolotan-Osman) that holds gas reserves of 16 trillion cubic feet. From the field, the pipeline will run to Herat and Kandahar provinces of Afghanistan before entering Pakistan. In Pakistan, it will reach Multan via Quetta before ending at Fazilka (Punjab) in India. The annual pumping capacity of the gas pipeline will be 33 billion cubic meters per years (bcm/y) of which India and Pakistan would each receive 14bcm/y while Afghanistan will get 5bcm/y (Azer News, 2015).

Thirdly, growing regional instability in Afghanistan, emanating from religious extremism and terrorism is another point of convergence between India and CARs. To an extent security and stability of Afghanistan is linked to security and stability of India as well as CARs. The drawdown of foreign troops from Afghanistan and consolidation of Islamic State (IS) in the border areas of Afghanistan has added a new dimension in the security landscape of the region. To prevent Afghanistan from becoming the hub of extremism and terrorism is the common goal of India and CARs. They can work together through bilateral and multilateral initiatives to establish peace in Afghanistan and ensure security and stability in the entire region. In fact, India has signed the Joint Working Group (JWG) mechanism on counter-terrorism and has signed various defence agreements with them to strengthen security (Roy, 2017: 96-97). India also conducts joint military exercises with them to boost their military capabilities.

Russia as a Facilitator in India and Central Asia Relations

Central Asian region has always been considered as the 'Strategic Backyard' of Russia, because they have an 'umbilical cord' with Russia. Therefore, Russia will always remain a key factor with any business in the Central Asian republics. Although in recent years, Russia's firm grip has loosened and China's growing energy needs prompted Beijing to look towards the Central Asian region. A global view of the overall geo-strategic situation will bring forward the following points concerning Russia: Russia is currently under sanctions and is suffering economically. Its military engagement in Syria, Ukraine and Crimea is also sapping it. To counter the US and prevent the world from turning into a unipolar hegemony, Russia is turning towards China. It is also looking towards China to alleviate its economic hardships. This effectively means that Russia defers to China in most cases and the Russian interests or real-politik might not necessarily align with Indian interests.

But at the same time the current international scenario is witnessing lots of regional and global complexities, where both the tendencies—cooperation and competition have become apparent among nations. Therefore, an element of competition between Russia and China is also visible (Joshi and Sharma, 2017: 44-49). It is against this background we need to question whether Russia will act as a facilitator in India-Central Asia relations. The answer is yes, because one can find an element of competition between Russia and China in Central Asia. On the other hand, Russia does not consider India as a country with expansionist designs. Rather India has acquired a very positive image among Central Asian republics also. That is the reason that Russia was the main force behind India's membership as a Full member in Shanghai Cooperation Organisation. Both Russia and Central Asian republics saw India as 'balancer' in this organisation. Secondly, Indian and Russian collaboration in connectivity projects like INSTC and India's collaboration with Eurasian Economic Union are welcome steps to bridge the gaps between India and Central Asian republics. In the words of Rajiv Sikri (Former Indian Ambassador to Kazakhstan), "In order to protect and preserve its interests in the region, India has no alternative but to closely consult and cooperate with the other major powers who have interest and a presence in Central Asia…. that partner is India's old friend, Russia" (Foshko, 2012). He further added that, "Some efforts need to be made for this partnership to work. The India-Russia bilateral relationship, while positive, has suffered from benign neglect and the two are currently passive allies in the region, sharing the same goals of stability and security yet not cooperating on specific projects" (Foshko, 2012).

Conclusion

India's renewed approach towards the region has acquired a new focus in its current foreign policy calculus. The factors and partnerships with regional countries, mentioned above, may help India in achieving its goals in the Central Asian region. Although the progress has been slow and fulfilment of some of the projects may seem doubtful, it must be underlined that the success and failure of a project depends upon the environment in which it works. There exists many geo-strategic challenges that India will have to navigate, but India's initiatives in the new emerging landscape, offer opportunities as well, to carve its own space within the Central Asian landscape. In this endeavour, India's membership to Shanghai Cooperation Organisation is another significant step. Since India and Pakistan joined this multi-lateral forum together where Russia and China have been highly active, India needs to use this forum for its proactive policies of connectivity in question. However, India's active participation in all the meetings of the organisation has increased its visibility as well as diplomatic investment in the region that was considered to be missing in the past. Moreover, setting up of a new mechanism of India–Central Asia Dialogue at the ministerial level is another move to institutionalise the relationship. In its first meeting which was held in Samarkand (Uzbekistan) on 12-13 January 2019, India's Minister of External Affairs Ms. Sushma Swaraj had already highlighted that, "India has always been and will always be a reliable friend and partner of Central Asia. The time has come to substantially raise our level of engagement" (Ministry of External Affairs, Government of India, 2019) and proposed definitive ideas on enhancing the level of engagement between India and Central Asia (Ministry of External Affairs, Government of India, 2019). The importance of this mechanism lies in the fact that no other major regional or global player is involved in this grouping. Hence, India and CARs can focus bilaterally on the areas of mutual interest and chalk out their future plans and strategies.

The fact that India has a strong cultural and emotional connect with the region that goes beyond the time of conceptualisations of geographical connectivity projects, the above-mentioned initiatives can help in making this connect stronger in the light of current developments. India has increasingly been seen as a balancer with no expansionist designs. There has been a substantial increase in the high-profile visits from both the sides. This momentum needs to be maintained. The proper follow-up and timely implementation of projects/initiatives undertaken will, no doubt, help in realising India's vision of Connect-Central Asia.

References

"ADB to attract funds for TAPI project". http://azernews.az/business/88688.html. (accessed:12 December, 2016), Also see, "TAPI Pipeline: India asks Turkmenistan to ease rules". articles.economictimes.indiatimes.com/2015-02-11/news/59043581_1_tapi-project-gas-pipeline-project-tapi-pipeline. (accessed:12.12. 2016)

Bandyopadhyaya, J. (1979). The Making of India's Foreign Policy. New Delhi, Allied Publishers.

Bhattacherjee, K. (October 29, 2017). "India ships wheat to Afghanistan via Chabahar". The Hindu, New Delhi.

Bohr, A. (March 2016). "Turkmenistan: Power, politics and Petro – Authoritarianism." http://ww.chathamhouse.org/sites/files/chathamhouse/publications/research/2016-03-08-turkmenistan-bohr.pdf (accessed: 13.12. 2016)

Brezezinski, Z. (1997). The Grand Chessboard: American Primacy and its Geostrategic Imperatives. New York, Basic Books.

Choudhary,D.R. "INSTC draft approval: Big Step Forward on India-Iran-Russia Corridor". economictimes.indiatimes.com/news/politics-and-nations/instc-draft-approval-big-step-forward-on-india-iran-russia-corridor/articles/ow/48766349.cms. (accessed: 20.10. 2016)

Choudhury, D.R. (March 26, 2018). "Uzbekistan seeks to be India's all-weather ally in Central Asia", The Economic Times. New Delhi.

Fettweis,C. J.(Spring 2015). On Heartlands and Chessboards: Classical Geopolitics, Then and Now. Orbis, 59 (2). p.233

Fettweis, C.J. (Summer 2000). "Sir Halford Mackinder, Geopolitics, and Policymaking in the 21st Century". Parameters. xxx (2). p. 58.

Foshko, K. "India and Russia: a new Central Asian engagement". http://www.gatewayhouse.in/india-and-russia-new-central-asian-engagement/. (accessed: 25.07. 2018)

Ikenberry, G.J. (November-December 2012). "The Revenge of Geography- Capsule Review". Foreign Affairs. http://www.foreignaffairs.com/reviews/capsule-review/revenge-geography. (accessed: 30.06.2018)

"India supports developing Chabahar port as alternate access route to Afghanistan, Central Asia: MEA", (March 15, 2018), Indian Express. http://indianexpress.com/article/india/india-supports-developing-chabahar-port-as-alternate-access-route-to-afghanistan-central-asia-mea-50989748. (accessed:16.03.2018)

"India Joins the Ashgabat Agreement". (February 01, 2018). Ministry of External Affairs, Government of India. Retrieved from, mea.gov.in/press-releases.htm dtl/29406/india_Joins_the_Ashgabat_Agreement. (accessed: 20.02. 2018)

"India takes over operations of part of Chabahar Port in Iran", Press Information Bureau, Government of India. http://pib.nic.in/newsite/PrintRelease.aspx?relid=187242. (accessed: 26.02. 2019)

"India-Uzbekistan ink Pacts to boost Cooperation", (July 07, 2015). The Hindu, ww.thehindu.com/news/national/prime-minister-narendra-modi-visit-to-uzbekistan/article/7392482.ece. (accessed: 12.05. 2016)

"India to Accede to Ashgabat Agreement", http:/.pib.nic.in/newsite/printrelease.aspx? rclid=138309.(accessed: 12.05. 2016)

"International North-South Transport Corridor (INSTC)-Dry Run Report 2014". commerce.nic.in/publications/INSTC-Dry-run-report-Final.pdf. (accessed: 20.10. 2016)

Joshi, N., Sharma, R.K. (2017), "India Russia Relations in a changing Eurasian Perspective", India Quarterly.73(1), pp. 44–9.

Kang, G.S., Won, Y. "Eurasian Economic Integration and Regional Connectivity", https://www.researchgate.net/publication/311707061_Eurasian_Economic_Integration_and_Regional_Connectivity.(accessed: 18.02. 2019)

Kaplan's interview, "How Geography Informs the Fate of the World". http://www.npr.org/templates/transcript/transcript.php?story Id=161087606.(accessed: 30.06. 2018)

"Kazakhstan eyes Terminal at Mundra to give fillip to Bilateral trade". www.thestatesman.com/news/business/Kazakhstan-eyes-terminal-at-mundra-to-give-fillip-to-bilateral-trade/106535.html.(accessed: 19.10. 2016)

Klare, M.T., Engelhardt, T. (June 16, 2006). "The Tripolar Chessboard", Tom Dispatch. cited in Dietl, G. (2017). India and the Global Game of Gas Pipelines, London and New York, Routledge, p. 57

Linn, J.F. "Central Asian Regional Integration and Cooperation: Reality or Mirage?". https://www.brookings.edu/wp-content/uploads/2016/06/10-regional-integration-and-cooperation-linn.pdf. (accessed: 27.08.2017)

Lopour, J. (November 2015). "Geopolitics at the World's Pivot: Exploring Central Asia's Security Challenges", CIGI Papers No. 80. p. 2.

Menashri, D. (1998). Central Asia Meets the Middle East, Frank Cass, London, cited in Dietl, G. (2017). India and the Global Game of Gas Pipelines, London and New York. Routledge, p. 57

Putz, C. (December 06, 2017). "Ghani and Mirziyoyev Meet, Renew Afghan-Uzbek Ties", The Diplomat. http://the diplomat.com/2017/12/ghani-and-mirziyoyev-meet-renew-afghan-uzbek-ties/. (accessed: 21.12.2017)

Rad, A.R.F. (2012). "Examining the TAPI Pipeline and its Impact on Regional and Cross – Regional Rivalry," Central Asia and the Caucasus, 13(2), pp. 83-84.

Roy, M.S., Roy, R. (October 2017). "Placing India in the Emerging Regional Dynamic of Central Asia", UNISCI Journal. no. 5. pp. 96-97.

Sanghera, B., Satybaldieva, E. "Central Asia is the new economic battleground for the US, China and Russia". http://theconversation.com/central-asia-is-the-new-economic-battleground-for-the-us-china-and-russia-98263. (accessed: 07.03.2019)

Saran, S. (June 08, 2018). "The Revenge of History: Eurasia rises". https://www.orfonline.org/expert-speak/41456-the-revenge-of-history-eurasia-rises/. (accessed: 07.03. 2019)

Sekhani, R. "What does the FTA with EEU has in store for India?". http://www.financialexpress.com/fe- columnist/what-does-the-fta-with eeu-has -in-store-for- india/90167/. (accessed : 13.10. 2016)

Sempa, F.P. (Fall 2015). "The Roots of Mackinder's Geopolitics". Orbis. 59(4), p. 613.

Sharma Hriday Ch., Menezes Dwayne R (June 06, 2018) "International North-South Transport Corridor (INSTC): India's Grand Plan for Northern Connectivity", http://polarconnection.org/india-instc-nordic-arctic/ (accessed: 11.10. 2018)

Stobdan, P. (December 12, 2017). "To make Chabahar a 'Game Changer' Central Asian states need to be roped in", IDSA Comment. http://idsa.in/idsacomments/to-make-chabahar-a-game-changer-central-asian_states_pstobdan_121217. (accessed:12.12. 2017)

"Tej Kadam: India-Kazakhstan Joint Statement. mea-gov.in/outgoing-visit-detail.htm? /Tej+Kadam+India+Kazakhstan+joint+statement. (accessed: 12.06. 2016)

"Statement by External Affairs Minister at the First Session of the India-Central Asia Dialogue", Ministry of External Affairs, Government of India. https://www.mea.gov.in/Speeches-Statements.htm?dtl/30905/Statement+by+External+Affairs+Minister+at+the+First+Session+of+the+IndiaCentral+Asia+Dialogue. (accessed: 25 .02. 2019)

FOUR

The Importance of India for Multi-Vector Foreign Policy of Kyrgyzstan

Halim Nezihoglu

Introduction

After the emergence of independent Central Asian republics, which remained under the rule of Tsarist Russian and successor Soviet empire for several decades, Central Asia has become an arena for great power rivalry. It was a rational choice for newly independent Kyrgyzstan, as a small country, neighbour to giant China, and whose dependency on Russia continued to a certain degree for security reasons and economic considerations, to adopt a multi-vector foreign policy in order to decrease its dependency on the former overlord and to counterbalance its giant neighbour which pursued expansionist policy in trade and the other projects in the region. In accordance with such a rationality, Kyrgyzstan, while keeping its relations with Russia and opening its borders for goods from China, also developed its relations with the US, Canada, EU, Germany, Turkey, Japan, etc., and became a member of several global or regional governmental organizations to integrate into global political and economic system. Though it's a relatively weaker role and influence in Central Asia compared to the other great powers, India, which never pursued an imperialist policy in the region in history, might be an important alternative option with regard to its huge demographic, economic, and technological capacity, geographical proximity, and historical-cultural links for foreign policy orientation of Kyrgyzstan.

India, with its huge potential to be a great counterweight, can make multi-vector foreign policy of Kyrgyzstan more successful, sustainable, and well-balanced, by providing it with a new direction and dimension and more room for manoeuvring; so that, Kyrgyzstan will be able to create a more favourable, freer, safer, and less-restraining external setting to conduct its foreign policy as an independent and sovereign country.

Foreign Policies of Weaker States in relation to Great Powers

A foreign policy analysis (see Morin & Paquin, 2018; Alden & Aran, 2017; Hudson, 2014; Breuning, 2007) focuses on the framework of several internal and external factors interacting at individual/national/international levels which shape outcomes of foreign-policy decision-making processes of countries. Foreign policy analysis involves the study of making and implementation of foreign policy, and theoretical and methodological approaches to understand the underlying structures which shape foreign policies. Foreign policy of a country, as the sum total of its actions and policies toward and interactions with the other countries in its region and in the world, is formed not only by the preferences and tendencies of the internal actors (such as leaders, government, bureaucracy, lobbies, interest groups, media, public opinion, etc.) but also by the influence and constraints of the regional and international actors (such as the other states—regional or great powers—and institutional/legal norms, mechanisms, and institutions in an international context). So, a foreign policy analysis has both internal/domestic and regional/international dynamics and dimensions. Options for the leaders and other internal actors are constrained not only by the conditions of regional milieu and global setting but historical, cultural, geopolitical context, and economic and military capacity of the country as well. History, national identity, self/other perceptions, political culture, geopolitics, and other inherent domestic dynamics of a country are basic determinants which form generalised notions and attitudes, and strategic mentality of the decision makers. Moreover, foreign policy objectives are constrained by the power of the country, defined by its geographic and demographic size, natural resources, and technological, industrial, economic, and military capabilities. However, an efficient use of these capabilities by an effective leadership, strategic planning, and skilful diplomacy will have a multiplier effect in bringing power potential of a country to fruition. The combination of all these factors and their efficient use or non-use define the posture of a country in its regional environment, and sets its position among the society of states. According to their status in international environment, countries are classified as small, middle, and regional or great powers. The distribution of power in a regional or international system, the position of a country in the systemic structure, and the impact of basic parameters of the system on a country define the contours of that country's foreign policy.

A small country's weak posture generally leads to asymmetrical patterns of relations with great powers and creates dependency. A weak state is likely to comply with the desires of a great power because it lacks resources to act independently. Seeking cooperation with a great power is more likely when weaker state cannot create a counter-balance by aligning with the other powers against the great power. Stable, long-lasting or slowly changing basic parameters of a regional or international political system provide guiding principles and outlines for foreign-policy makers of a member of the society of states (see Breuning, 2007: 149–56). In shaping grand strategies as overall survival strategies of states, weaker states suffer from systemic vulnerabilities given their underdevelopment, shortage of capabilities, and lack of power. Weak states avoid sanctions or other types of threats from great powers; rather, they seek to ensure against their security and survival being threatened. So, they try to comply with the policies of the great powers and get financial aid or other types of economic assistance from them. Assistance by great powers for economic development, international trade, and security from threats such as terrorism, drug-trafficking, environmental disasters, global financial fluctuations, and other global challenges is vital for weak states. These vital needs for survival increase their vulnerability to the influence of the great powers and dependence on them. Geographical proximity, location of the weak state within the historical zone of influence of a great power, and other security-related, political, and economic linkages further increase this dependency. Great powers are motivated to keep this dependency because weak states are important for them to increase their power, prestige, and wealth. If possible, weak states prefer to diversify the partners to develop relations with, instead of remaining loyal to only one power, in order to decrease the dependency, to create greater room for manoeuvring, and to gain more benefits such as aid from and preferential trade agreements with as many countries as possible. By playing the field, it might be possible for weak states to play the great powers off against one another as a type of soft-balancing to maximise their benefits with lowest costs (see Kassab, 2018: 1-12, 34-38). Lack of power to cope with not only external threats but also internal threats such as rebellions and popular revolutions motivates the ruling elite of a weak state to align with great powers in order to safeguard the survival of their leadership regime. Weaker states seek cooperation and form an internal threat alliance with great powers because they need military or economic resources to eliminate challenges inside the country to their existence (Quirk, 2017: 11, 12). Thus, weaker states prefer cooperation and alliance to conflict in their relations with great powers. However, weaker states try to diversify partners for cooperation and alternative allies in order to minimise the disadvantages and unfavourable circumstances of asymmetrical nature of interactions between the weaker and the great.

Foreign policy diversification or multi-vector foreign policy seems to be the best foreign policy strategy for weaker states to adopt, especially if they are located in a region vulnerable to the influence(s) of great power(s) and in an arena open to great power rivalry because of geopolitical and other reasons. Weak states, having a market-type rationality, get involved in a multi-vector diplomacy to attract a variety of actors in different issue-areas or in their more particular components where assistance is needed. The domination and monopoly of one power in all areas make the weak state totally dependent on the assistance of that state; and so, it minimises benefits while maximising costs as it leaves no room for autonomy and manoeuvring. Rivalry and competition between great powers on different interest-areas in the region decreases the pressure over the weak state, because one power counterbalances another; and provides room for autonomy and choice among alternative options. Central Asian states, situated in a great power-driven regional system, adopted such a diversification policy as an overall foreign policy strategy. Because of the enduring Soviet legacies and Russian imperial economic design in landlocked Central Asia, such as regional integration mechanisms, through which Russia defined the rules of the game, and Russian-centreed industrial infrastructure and transport network, which make Russia pre-eminent and dominant power in the region, the republics were left with no option but to turn to multi-vectorism in order to mitigate the costs of dependency inherent in core-periphery relations. The rise and return of Russia in the region further motivated the republics to hold multi-vector policy in high regard. Though Russia has kept its pre-eminent role in the region since the collapse of the Soviet Union, the republics have sought to develop good relations and cooperation with different global/regional powers and other states, and to balance diverse interests of various players. Multi-vector diplomacy, which 'implies the simultaneous co-alignment with different great powers', has become the guiding principle for the formulation and implementation of foreign policy of the Central Asian and many other post-Soviet republics. As it seems to be the only way or the most effective way to reduce dependency on Russia, it has become a fundamental and strategic approach to statecraft rather than a temporary tactic in the region. It provides them with room for relational power in different issue-areas and autonomy; increases their bargaining power with competing states over the terms of cooperation; and helps them preserve sovereignty in asymmetric relationship. In the global arena or marketplace of foreign relations and state-to-state cooperation, the availability of alternative powers, competition between them, and multi-polarity work to the advantage of weaker states (Contessi, 2018: 1-7; 2015: 299-302).

Great Powers and New Players in Central Asia

Central Asia, which remained under the Tsarist Russian and then the Soviet rule for more than a century, became an arena for great power rivalry, also referred as 'new great game', after the dissolution of the Soviet Union because of several reasons such as the region's geopolitical importance, rich energy resources, strategic considerations and competitions of great powers and their motives to take the benefits of new opportunities created by the collapse of the union. Either similar or diversified motives have stimulated great powers to develop relations with the newly independent republics and to increase their influences in the region. While Russia wanted to reintegrate the region under its leadership to strengthen its declined position and not to lose the area to its rivals, China expanded its trade by reviving Silk Road through transportation projects and sought to consume energy resources through energy projects. The US, pursuing a global strategy, aimed at checking and counterbalancing China and Russia through military airbases, seeking security cooperation in its post-9/11 war on terror, promoting liberal democracy, and increasing its soft power through educational and cultural projects. Not only great powers but also other countries around the region sought to enhance their presence in the region through attempts in different areas such as trade, business, investment, finance, education, culture, religious activities, etc.

In accordance with the rise of Eurasianist ideas among the Russian intellectual circles in the 1990s and then in political circles and larger public space in the 2000s, as a vision of reunion of the Eurasian space under the umbrella of Russia, with an inherent belief that Eurasia is a unique region different from the West and should reject the western imperialism (see Laruelle, 2008: 1-12; 2004: 115-117; Nezihoglu & Sayın, 2013: 375-379), Putin pursued an ambitious policy to revive the leading role of Russia in the Near Abroad through institutional integration mechanisms such as CIS, Eurasian Customs Union, and Eurasian Union. Through Eurasian Customs Union, Russia wanted to make Russian manufactured goods dominate the regional market by raising tariffs against goods imported from non-members of Eurasian Economic Union. After the Russians suffered from a trauma of losing a great empire and one of the two superpowers of the Cold War era in the 1990s, Putin and the Russian ruling elite began to pursue policies to return Russia to its lost glory after the 2000s. In conformity with the motto 'Russia is back', Putin has aimed to bring about a powerful, dominant, and globally respected great Russia (McNabb, 2016: 3-15). A conception of 'Great Russia' and an imperial strategic perspective, inherent in Russian national identity and the Russian view of the Near Abroad, confirm that Russia is the only dominant power in the region and that the Near Abroad is an area where Russian vital interests should be protected (see Laenen, 2012: 17-32). Having a loyal and dependent Near Abroad, willing to support Russia's foreign policy and strategic interests, is important for Russia to view itself truly as a great power. So, post-Soviet countries around Russia keep top priority in Russian foreign policy and strategic interests (Nalbandov, 2016: 194-195). Moreover, decades-long Russian domination, territorial proximity, its military operational capacity in Eurasia and Central Asia, and its guarantor role against security challenges such as border conflicts and ethnic tensions put Russia in a more advantageous position versus the other players. Common historical and linguistic links, entrenched habits and shared perceptions among the ruling elites of the region, demographic and economic considerations, security anxieties, and other challenges are the motivating factors for the republican leaders to be part of this regional reunion under Russian leadership.

China is a rising giant, perceived by many to have a potential to rise to a global hegemonic power, with its rising assertiveness in recent decades. China, as a demographic, economic and financial giant, is likely to seek its geopolitical ambitions and to expand its influence in its region and in the world in accordance with its growing economic, financial, technological and military power and capacity. After the disintegration of the Soviet Union, China sought to develop its relations and cooperation with the Central Asian republics for such purposes as the maintenance of security along its western borders, the diversification of energy supplies to meet its huge need, economic development of its western region, expansion of the export market for its manufactured products, security cooperation against terrorism and separatism; and accordingly, signed bilateral economic and trade agreements with them. Furthermore, China took the lead in founding Shanghai Cooperation Organization in 2001 as an institutionalised mechanism for regional cooperation with the aims of trade facilitation by removal of non-tariff barriers and investment in transport and energy (Cheng, 2017: 384-389). Since 2013, Chinese President Xi Jinping has been promoting the BRI (The Belt and Road Initiative), also known as the OBOR (The One Belt, One Road) strategy as a major diplomatic initiative. The first part of the land-based route of this great project, with the aim of the building of Silk Road Economic Belt as a transportation, economic and energy network which would link China and Central Asia closely, is a strategic vision in Chinese foreign policy toward Central Asia. China has invested and will continue to spend billions of dollars to build new transport infrastructures such as highways, railroads, and pipelines and to upgrade the existing ones in order to realise this strategy. China as an important creditor and economic partner with its profitable projects also signed strategic partnership agreements with Central Asian republics (see Indeo, 2018: 135-149; Danner, 2018: 30, 78).

The US as a global power, the main rival of Russia both in the cold war-era bipolar world order and in the post-cold war-era tensions of transition to a new world order, has engaged in developing her ties with Central Asian republics after the collapse of the Soviet Union. Central Asia's geopolitics, predominantly shaped by its landlocked location between Russia and China and its proximity to Afghanistan, made the region and the maintenance of access to airspace and solid ground of the region vitally important for the US global strategy. The US sought to promote liberalisation and democratisation in this post-Soviet region; supported the integration of the republics into global society of states, global organizations, and global economy; tried to keep open access to Central Asian market; and supported alternative pipeline projects which would bypass Russia. Especially after the 9/11 terror attacks in 2001, the US attached greater importance to the region, in accordance with its 'global war on terror' strategy which required the maintenance of stability in the region, neighbour to Afghanistan. Democracy promotion in the region was regarded as a vital interest by the US ruling elite in order to prevent instabilities, societal turmoil, and radicalism, mostly led by authoritarian misrule of the governments, political repression, rampant corruption, widening socio-economic inequalities, and poverty (Blank, 2007: 312-315).

In addition to these great powers, numerous actors such as EU, Germany, Turkey, Japan, Korea, Iran, Arab countries, and other countries from different regions tried to develop their relations with the republics in different spheres such as trade or educational, cultural, and other areas. Though the US and China have prudently avoided to irritate and agitate Russia in their attempts to develop their relations and cooperation with Central Asian republics in the Russian Near Abroad, it should be noted that the presence of different powers and players in the region pose a counterbalance against the monopoly of Russia and against each other. Competition between diverse actors and a finely tuned balance between them keep going to the exclusion of hegemony and monopoly of one power and so provide more capability for Central Asian republics to establish their sovereignty, to pursue autonomous policies, to maximise their interests by having more room for external balancing and manoeuvrability. Absence of alternative powers in the region would make the republics totally dependent on their former overlord and leave the region to the initiatives of one power only.

Multi-vector Foreign Policy of Kyrgyzstan

Central Asian republics have pursued multi-vectorism as their general foreign policy orientation, though in varying degrees (see Hanks, 2009: 259-267; Minasyan, 2012; Diyarbakirlioglu and Yigit, 2014). Kyrgyzstan has also adopted multi-vector foreign policy since its independence and tried to develop its ties with different countries although Russia has kept priority in foreign relations of the young republic. Post-Soviet period created fresh opportunities for newly independent Kyrgyz Republic, in urgent need for development assistance and investment from foreign allies in different fields when the disintegration of the union attracted alternative players to the region, to develop cooperation with new partners in a new and challenging regional and global environment. The first President Akaev and Kyrgyz authorities welcomed the involvement of new players in their foreign relations when the country was struggling to cope with challenges of the collapse of the union and trying to transit into free market economy and to integrate into international society of states as an independent actor. In order to renew its outmoded infrastructure, to have alternative providers and supply chains to satisfy ever-growing demands of the people in the new free market conditions, to attract foreign assistance, financial aid, and investment in areas within urgent need of development, to maintain economic survival without subsidies from Moscow, and to maximise its national interests, Kyrgyzstan rationally took the advantage of the availability of multiple alternative collaborators and supporters; and so, it sought to diversify the new partners for cooperation.

Kyrgyzstan, as the most liberal-democratic country among Central Asian republics, kept its doors open to diverse players. Persistent authoritarianism in the greater region surrounding Kyrgyzstan, defined as 'island of democracy' by numerous analysts, makes democracy and friendly relations with major regional and global actors the most valuable asset of the country which is comparatively poor in energy resources. In the 1990s, Kyrgyzstan signed a number of bilateral agreements with different countries and multilateral treaties with different organizations; and became a member of major global and regional organizations such as United Nations (UN), Organization for Security and Cooperation in Europe (OSCE), World Trade Organization (WTO), World Bank, International Monetary Fund (IMF), Asian Development Bank (ADB), Organization of Islamic Cooperation (OIC), Commonwealth of Independent States (CIS), Shanghai Cooperation Organization (SCO), etc. Kyrgyzstan also joined the North Atlantic Cooperation Council, a forum for dialogue in NATO, in 1992, and NATO Partnership for Peace program in 1994, which allowed the education of Kyrgyz military cadres in NATO countries. Kyrgyzstan has received financial aids, technical equipment, economic assistance, know-how and training supports, investments, and grants from different agencies and donors such as European Bank for Reconstruction and Development (EBRD), The United States Agency for International Development (USAID), The Soros Foundation-Kyrgyzstan (SFK), Turkish International Cooperation and Development Administration (TIKA), Japan International Cooperation Agency (JICA), Korea International Cooperation Agency (KOICA), etc. These donors and agencies funded important projects and contributed much to the social and economic development of the country. The global variety and diversity of the organizational memberships and multiplicity of foreign engagements prove political will and strategic orientation of the Kyrgyz ruling elite toward multi-vector foreign policy. In spite of two popular revolutions—in 2005 and 2010—which replaced presidents and governments with new ones, multi-vectorism as general underlying principle of Kyrgyz foreign policy has been maintained under the rule of different Presidents: Akaev, Bakiev, Otunbayeva, Atambaev and Jeenbekov (see Sarı, 2012: 137-146).

Instead of sticking foreign policy to one direction in a fixed manner, Kyrgyzstan maintained many-sidedness, diverse transaction channels, openness, pragmatism, and flexibility in its foreign engagements; and pursued a sensitive balance within multiplicity of directions. Although the rising roles of Russia and to a certain degree China in the region in recent years make Kyrgyz leadership more cautious and prudent in their foreign policy discourse and attempts, there is no change in the fundamental multi-vector foreign policy strategy. While Russia and China are trying to shift the balance in favour of their strategic interests in the region and to dominate the area to the detriment of their rivals by taking advantages of their geographical proximity and other capabilities, Central Asian republics in general and Kyrgyzstan in specific have a rising need to develop cooperation with alternative powers in order to consolidate the counterbalance and to keep the sensitive balance.

India and Central Asia

Great power rivalry for creating zones of influence in Central Asia and growing involvement of multiple actors in the region pose challenges to and impose responsibilities on India in its strategy towards its extended neighbourhood—greater inner Asia, in other words. India as an emerging power with its huge demographic, economic, and technological capacity cannot be expected to remain 'an indifferent onlooker' and to be unresponsive to the shifts in geopolitical balance in Central Asia, which would have great consequences for the strategic outlook of the country in its northern tier (Kavalski, 2010: 3,4). Cold War era had provided a stable and predictable order with Indian foreign strategy. However, post-Cold War era created an environment of uncertainties and radical transformations in greater Central Asian region which required a new formulation of the country's foreign policy towards the north. It seems to be necessary for India to help maintain stability in the region as an active player and to prevent rising security risks and challenges such as terrorism and militant Islam after the collapse of the Soviet Union which had been a security manager and guarantor. The region is strategically and geopolitically important for India because of the fact that the region is a bridge on the traditional silk road with Russia and the Middle East; it has huge energy reserves at relatively short distance, vital for Indian industrial growth; it might be an important market for Indian growing export industries; and more importantly, it is a crucial area which cannot be abandoned to uncertainties and instabilities or to the ambitions of the other powers so as to prevent encirclement by a great challenging power or one of India's rivals, for example China or an Islamic belt allied to Pakistan (see Moore, 2007: 279-289). Diplomatic relations and volume of trade are ever increasing between India and Central Asian republics as they signed numerous agreements. However, greater trade potential between them might be fully achieved if political and economic stability in Central Asia, Afghanistan, and Pakistan is assured with cooperative relationships between these countries and India on the basis of an inclusive win-win approach (see Malik, 2014: 54-56, 66-68).

India's involvement in Central Asia would strengthen its posture towards China, Russia, the West, and Pakistan. Although India avoided aggressive power politics in its political history, the need for the maintenance of peace, order, and stability in its extended neighbourhood, to which it has geographical proximity, historical and cultural links, requires it to increase its role and engagement in the region which includes Pakistan, Afghanistan, and Central Asia. The 1962 war between India and China was a decisive moment which introduced a deep psychological change in India's leadership and foreign-policy bureaucracy from Nehru's fixed loyalty to peace, anti-military orientation, and a no-war policy with China. This war awakened the ruling elite of India about China's ambitions; and so they began to recognize the need to revise foreign policy towards China, to make major changes in their national security notion and planning, and in the country's military and economic capacity (Kapur, 2011: 135-141). India's defeat in the war further encouraged New Delhi to develop its own nuclear weapons to deter Chinese aggression. The 1998 nuclear tests, seen by many analysts as a tectonic shift in Indian foreign strategy and a decisive break with its traditional commitment to peace diplomacy, increased self-assurance in India and assertiveness in its foreign policy. By building up its military and nuclear capacity and by adopting a new strategic notion and foreign policy paradigm, based on the realities of geopolitics and national interests, India emerged as a major power in the late 1990s (Kapur, 2006: 197-208; Kavalski, 2010: 37-45). While several players are actively getting involved in Central Asia, India has come to realise that it cannot refrain from considering its vital interests in its strategic neighbourhood. So, its foreign policy makers and scholars began to emphasise 'Look-North' policy (see Kavalski, 2010: 79-101) in terms of an increased engagement in Central Asia with which it has long-standing historical ties with cultural, social, religious, and economic dimensions.

Increasing confrontation between the West and Russia is likely to lead the latter to perceive India as a partner rather than rival if their long-lasting friendly relations during Cold War era are considered as well. Shared perceptions about challenging security risks such as the rise of

Islamic fundamentalism in Central Asia, Afghanistan, and Pakistan also bring Russia and India together. The two countries signed the Declaration on Strategic Partnership in October 2000, during Putin's visit to India. Friendly relations between them have gained an institutionalised character through the body of the Indo-Russian Inter-Governmental Commission and annual ministerial-level defence meetings. Absence of rivalry and confrontation between India and Russia, the primary and key player in Central Asia, is an encouraging factor which makes the leaders of Central Asian republics feel less restrained in developing their relations with India. In spite of the strategic cooperation between New Delhi and Moscow in certain shared interests, there are areas as well where their interests do not converge. In such areas such as energy, India might be regarded as an alternative to Russia. On the other side, the inclusion of India to the arena on which Russo–Chinese strategic alliance is noticeable lessen the solidarity of these three players because of discord and lack of trust between New Delhi and Beijing so as to provide more room for Central Asian republics to manoeuvre. The rise of China as an assertive global power is viewed by India with suspicion and anxiety while the rise of India as an Asian nuclear power would unease China. So, these powers might be considered as rivals or alternatives in the new great game over Central Asia. Although they have shared interests in preventing the rise of Islamic fundamentalism in the region, it should be noted that China supported Pakistan's development of nuclear and missile technology and became the biggest supplier of its conventional weapons (Kavalski, 2010: 139,140). The 1962 military conflict between two powers, border disputes, incursions of Chinese troops across the borders, the Sino-Pak alliance, India's support of the Dalai Lama, Chinese expansionist strategy in Asia, and Chinese fear of encirclement by a possible alliance between the US and India created a deep mutual mistrust which poisons their relations and prevents the rise of a strategic partnership between them. In Central Asia, regarded by both as a strategic area for their geopolitical and energy interests, rivalry rather than cooperation is more likely to dominate the relations between India and China (Huchet, 2010: 97-104, 111-113; see also Chaudhuri and Sethi, 2010: 123-129).

Conclusion

Unlimited and unchecked power leads to hegemony while absence of alternatives lead to monopolisation by one power in all areas. The presence and active involvement of multiple players in Central Asian arena provide alternative outlets and channels in multiple issues at multiple levels in foreign relations of the republics so as to navigate unreservedly and to better maximise their benefits. If the great powers and the other middle powers, as players in Central Asia, can reach a consensus and develop a joint effort in applying pressure over Central Asia, there will be no room for the republics to manoeuvre. However, though such a joint action might be possible in limited areas, divergent strategic calculations on the basis of realpolitik notions and clash of interests between them is likely to make them rivals in numerous issue-areas so as to create sufficient area for the republics to take action. So, an increase in the number and active involvement of diverse players in the region will further widen this controlling area and loosen the restraining pressure over the republics. Moreover, the multiplicity of the actors involved increases the possibility of shifting partnerships and building alliances and counter-alliances between them so that there will be more shelters available for the republics to seek support against any threat by one of the great powers.

India as a nuclear power with its huge demographic and economic capacity might be a considerable balancing factor in foreign relations of Kyrgyzstan against the other great powers. The pre-eminent role of Russia as the former overlord and the rising role of China in Central Asia make India one of the best alternatives among the other players in order to counter-balance their imperial strategies. Strong relations with India are expected to help minimise unfavourable conditions of Kyrgyzstan's weak posture against Russia, China, and the other powers, and so, to mitigate disadvantages of asymmetrical relations with them, and to decrease dependency on them. Having an alternative partner will increase the bargaining power of the country in the marketplace of foreign relations. The availability of more partners means more attainable sources and helping hands in meeting the country's needs for economic development and social progress. India, with its huge potential to be a great counterweight, can make multi-vector foreign policy of Kyrgyzstan more successful, sustainable, and well-balanced, by providing it with a new direction and dimension and more room for steering, so that Kyrgyzstan will be able to create a more favourable, freer, safer, and less-restraining external setting to conduct its foreign policy as an independent and sovereign country.

The importance of India stems from not only its role as a counter-balance but also its unique capacity to contribute to peaceful socio-political development in Kyrgyzstan. Without having an imperialist and aggressive foreign strategy in its history, India, with its pluralist democratic and stable secular regime in a multiethnic, multi-cultural and multi-religious, massive but peaceful society, have great experience of managing diversity and so capability to contribute to stable transition and peaceful social progress in Central Asia in general and Kyrgyzstan in specific. This aspect of India is a valuable asset for Kyrgyzstan as the most liberal-democratic country in a region dominated by authoritarianism. Persistent authoritarianism in the region make democracy in Kyrgyzstan not only precious but also fragile. Lack of a balanced economic growth, high rate of unemployment, financial shortages, corruption, and absence of a well-established ethnic cohesion at national level, when considered together with the two popular revolutions (2005 and 2010) which toppled the governments, and an ethnic conflict in 2010 since the independence of the country in 1991, make the fragility of democracy and ethnic harmony a serious risk and challenge. Thus, it is important for Kyrgyzstan and its government, in the vital need for the maintenance of security and the prevention of socio-economic instabilities, rebellions, social upheaval, and ethnic conflicts, to have alternative but reliable partners. On the other side, it is important for India to support peace, stability, regional cooperation, economic prosperity, and the prevention of ethnic conflicts and religious extremism in the region, because instabilities in its north beyond its borders will have negative consequences for its own multi-religious society, which includes a considerable number of Muslims. These realities make India one of the best alternative partners and supporters for a stable transition and peaceful social progress in Kyrgyzstan.

References

Alden, C., & Aran, A. (2017). Foreign Policy Analysis: New Approaches. London and New York: Routledge.

Blank, S. (2007). 'U.S. Interests in Central Asia and Their Challenges'. Demokratizatsiya, 15(3).

Breuning, M. (2007). Foreign Policy Analysis: A Comparative Introduction. New York: Palgrave Macmillan.

Chaudhuri, B. & Sethi, M. (2010). India-China Interactions in Central Asia through the Prism of Paul Kennedy's Analysis of Great Powers. In M. Laruelle, J-F Huchet, S. Peyrouse, and B. Balci (Eds.), China and India in Central Asia: A New "Great Game"? New York: Palgrave Macmillan.

Cheng, J. Y. (2017). Multilateral Approach in China's Foreign Policy.

DOI: 10.1142/9789813221116_0008

Contessi, N. P. (2015). 'Foreign and Security Policy Diversification in Eurasia: Issue-Splitting, Co-alignment, and Relational Power'. Problems of Post-Communism, 62(5). DOI:10.1080/10758216.2015.1026788

Contessi, N. P. (2018). 'Foreign Policy Diversification and Intercontinental Transport Corridors: The Case of Kazakhstan's Railway Diplomacy'. Europe-Asia Studies. DOI:10.1080/09668136.2018.1473342

Danner, L. K. (2018). China's Grand Strategy: Contradictory Foreign Policy? Cham, Switzerland: Palgrave Macmillan.

Diyarbakirlioglu, K. & Yigit, S. (2014). 'Kazakh Multi Vector Foreign Policy in Action'. **Alternatives** Turkish Journal of International Relations, 13(4), pp.70-82.

Hanks, R. R. (2009). 'Multi-vector Politics and Kazakhstan's Emerging Role as a Geo-Strategic Player in Central Asia'. Journal of Balkan and Near Eastern Studies, 11(3).

Huchet, J-F. (2010). India and China in Central Asia: Mirroring Their Bilateral Relations. In M. Laruelle, J-F Huchet, S. Peyrouse, and B. Balci (Eds.), China and India in Central Asia: A New "Great Game"? New York: Palgrave Macmillan.

Hudson, V. M. (2014). Foreign Policy Analysis: Classic and Contemporary Theory. Lanham, USA: Rowman & Littlefield.

Indeo, F. (2018). The Impact of the Belt and Road Initiative on Central Asia: Building New Relations in a Reshaped Geopolitical Scenario. In W. Zhang, I. Alon, and C. Lattemann (Eds.), China's Belt and Road Initiative: Changing the Rules of Globalization. Cham, Switzerland: Palgrave Macmillan.

Kapur, A. (2011). India and the South Asian Strategic Triangle. London and New York: Routledge.

Kapur, A. (2006). India – From Regional to World Power. London and New York: Routledge.

Kassab, H. S. (2018). Grand Strategies of Weak States and Great Powers. Cham, Switzerland: Palgrave Macmillan.

Kavalski, E. (2010). India and Central Asia: The Mythmaking and International Relations of A Rising Power. London & New York: I. B. Tauris Publishers.

Laenen, R. (2012). Russia's 'Vital and Exclusive' National Interests in the Near Abroad. In M. R. Freire & R. E. Kanet (Eds.), Russia and Its Near Neighbours: Identity, Interests and Foreign Policy (pp.17-38). London and New York: Palgrave Macmillan.

Laruelle, M. (2004). 'The Two Faces of Contemporary Eurasianism: An Imperial Version of Russian Nationalism'. Nationalities Papers, 32(1).

Laruelle, M. (2008). Rusian Eurasianism: An Ideology of Empire. Baltimore: The Johns Hopkins University Press.

Malik, I. A. (September-2014). 'India's Trade Potential with Central Asia: An Application of Gravity Model Analysis'. International Journal on World Peace, 7(3).

McNabb, D. E. (2016). Vladimir Putin and Russia's Imperial Revival. London and New York: CRC Press.

Minasyan, S. (2012). 'Multi-vectorism in the Foreign Policy of Post-Soviet Eurasian States'. Demokratizatsiya, 20(3), pp.268-273.

Moore, S. (June 2007). 'Peril and Promise: A Survey of India's Strategic Relationship with Central Asia'. Central Asian Survey, 26(2).

Morin, J. F., & Paquin, J. (2018). Foreign Policy Analysis: A Toolbox. Cham, Switzerland: Palgrave Macmillan.

Nalbandov, R. (2016). Not By Bread Alone: Russian Foreign Policy Under Putin. Nebraska: Potomac Books, The University of Nebraska Press.

Nezihoglu, H. & Sayın, F. M. (2013). 'Two Options among Numerous Directions: Eurasianism on Moscow's Terms or Regional Integration between Sovereign Neighbors in Central Asia'. The Journal of International Social Research, 6(26).

Quirk, P. W. (2017). Great Powers, Weak States, and Insurgency: Explaining Internal Threat Alliances. Cham, Switzerland: Palgrave Macmillan.

Sarı, Y. (2012). 'Foreign Policy of Kyrgyzstan under Askar Akaev and Kurmanbek Bakiev'. Perceptions, 17(3).

FIVE

Milieu of National Initiatives: Perspective on Cross Leveraging India and Central Asia Relations- A Case Study of Uzbekistan

Bilal Bhat

Introduction

The Central Asian States are born in the 20th century within the conceptual frame of ethnic nationalism (Hassan 1996: 2016). Islam Karimov, former president of Uzbekistan, maintains that his country is "the heart of Central Asia", and further explains: "Uzbekistan has been historically destined to be located on the crossroads of Eurasia, linking the West with the East, the South with the North. This enables us to advance the idea of the Republic providing in the long term a Eurasian economic and scientific cultural bridge similar to the Great Silk Road (Hassan 1996: 191)." The Uzbeks are daring, dashing and enterprising people whose tradition of obeying the authority and great love for their history and culture are great assets in their national character (Chandra 2015: 37).

While discussing Indo-Uzbek relations it is rather difficult to separate the past from the present. The past feeds and enriches the present and provides the ambience for warm relations that exist between the two countries. It was/is found quite essential to develop bilateral, trilateral and multi-lateral relations among the countries of the world and the region at large, and India, for instance, contributed to the regional cooperation as a strong ally (Mushtaq 2010: 375). Both India and China are new players in Central Asia's 'Great Game'(Economictimes.indiatimes.com, 2019).

To illustrate Indo-Uzbek bonds since ancient times, few examples are shared in this chapter. In the 11th century a great scientist and encyclopaedist Abu Raihon Al-Beruni travelled from Khiva to India. In his fundamental scientific work known under the title of India he has described the unique nature, history, philosophical-religious views and lifestyle of the Indian people. The Kitab-Tahkik Al-Hind is one of the most authoritative books on Indian society and culture. The socio-cultural relations further expanded and strengthened during the Moghul Dynasty (1526-1857) in India. Zahiruddin Muhammad Babur in his famous work of Baburname rediscovered the distant and mysterious India, and for Indian people the beauties of Uzbekistan homeland (MEA 2019).

Indo-Uzbek partnership for regional peace and stability is very important taking into account the historical background of the relationship, the current trends, areas of contention and cooperation, the challenges, prospects and implication. Lot of attention is required to examine the various components and dimensions of the relationship, and suggest ways to overcome the current stalemate. Steps have been taken to overcome radicalisation to be able to benefit from the resultant demographic dividend (Narayan, Tursonov and Kumar 2018, 15).

India, Central Asian nations back inclusive Afghan peace process

India and the five Central Asia nations of Uzbekistan, Kazakhstan, Kyrgyzstan, Tajikistan and Turkmenistan backed an inclusive peace process in Afghanistan that is Afghan-owned and Afghan-led following the first ever India–Central Asia Dialogue. External Affairs Minister Sushma Swaraj co-chaired the Dialogue that was also attended by the Foreign Ministers of Afghanistan, Uzbekistan, Kyrgyzstan, Tajikistan and Turkmenistan and the First Deputy Foreign Minister of Kazakhstan.

"India ... reiterates its support and commitment to peace, security and stability of Afghanistan; to promote inclusive Afghan-led, Afghan-owned and Afghan-controlled peace and reconciliation process and to assist in economic reconstruction of Afghanistan," she told the media after the Dialogue. "I pointed out that no business development, no investment can take place in a country suffering from terrorism," she said. "To promote business development in our region, we agreed to fight the scourge of terrorism together." Though New Delhi, as a policy, does not hold talks with the Taliban, it has indicated that it supports an inclusive peace process in Afghanistan. India and the US earlier discussed the on-going peace process in Afghanistan during a meeting between Sushma Swaraj and US President Donald Trump's Special Envoy on Afghanistan Zalmay Khalilzad. Khalilzad's visit for an intra-Afghan political settlement reflects New Delhi's stand that it is for an "Afghan-owned, Afghan-led and Afghan-controlled" peace and reconciliation process (Greater Kashmir 2019).

Commercial and Trade Relations

Trade relations between India and Uzbekistan are governed by the Agreement on Trade and Economic Cooperation signed in May 1993. This agreement provides for such things as promotion of economic, industrial, scientific and technical cooperation, including in the field of training of personnel, active participation of small and medium-sized enterprises in bilateral economic cooperation, and counter-trade, etc. India and Uzbekistan also signed an Agreement on Avoidance of Double Taxation in 1993 and for Bilateral Investment Promotion and Protection in May 1999. The Inter-Governmental Commission (IGC) has met nine times, and the last Session was held in Tashkent on 4 May 2011 (MEA 2019). On 15 April 2019, delegates from the Astana International Financial Centre (AIFC) and Observer Research Foundation, had a closed-door conference on the importance of strengthening bilateral relations between Kazakhstan and India. The talks were not only related to economic relations, but also encompassed how the two countries can combine efforts to ensure increased trade and connectivity in the changing geopolitical stances of the world. There have been several changes in the political landscape in the geography of Central Asia — with the entry of China as a major player in funding infrastructure projects in the region, and the weakening influence of USA in the markets, along with the independence from Soviet Union — Kazakhstan has had to emerge as a critical power in the Central Asia region. With this, Kazakhstan is now looking to increase its presence in Central Asia by fostering ties with

India to facilitate a North-South trade corridor. Thus, it is also important for India to look at Kazakhstan as a stepping stone into the markets of Central Asia and develop an outreach strategy to connect to Central Asia to compete with the growing presence of China in that region (orfonline 2019).

Today it can be said that trade and economic relations between Uzbekistan and India over the years have largely been very successful. For the past decade, the mutual trade turnover has grown by more than 12 times and in 2004 reached $120.9 million. But during the last year bilateral trade dropped to $61.1 million. The exports of Uzbekistan to India primarily consisted of aircraft, products of metallurgy, services, agriculture, silken and cotton textiles, and chemical industrial products apart from beans, silver, raw cotton and silk, pulses and services while imports from India comprised services, pharmaceuticals and medicines, machinery and equipment, organic and chemical products, optical equipment and devices, textiles and many more apart from drugs, paper, wood products, garments and fabrics, tea, plastic items, surgical items and consumer goods. There are currently 31 large enterprises in Uzbekistan, which have been established with the direct participation of Indian companies and investment: 26 of them are joint ventures and 5 are enterprises with 100 per cent Indian capital (Mushtaq 2012, 377). The most distinguished are the "The Diamond Uzbekistan International" (tourism), "Multi Channel Impex Limited" (cotton processing and commerce), and etc. These enterprises made valuable contribution to the development of Uzbekistan's pharmaceutical, tourism, construction and many other industries (Mushtaq 2012, 377). However, at the same time the current level of economic cooperation between the two countries does not meet its significant potential. The two countries surely have enormous opportunities to expand this cooperation in many areas (Doraswamy 2017, 5).

Science and technology are other areas of cooperation between Uzbekistan and India. A Working Programme in Science and Technology for 2004-2006 was signed in New Delhi in March 2004. This envisages joint workshops and conferences in areas of bilateral interest; exchange visits of scientific and technological personnel; training of young Uzbek scientists in Indian Institutions; and implementation of joint research projects in areas considered significant for the development of economy on both sides. Considerable scope for cooperation exists in the area of information technology in which Indian companies have made a mark for themselves on the global scale. Under the memorandum of understanding signed in October 2004 for establishing an Indo-Uzbek Centre for Information Technology in Tashkent, the government of India provided Uzbekistan with a grant of Rs 30 million, and also technical assistance. The building identified for the India-Uzbek IT Centre in The Tashkent University of Information Technology has been renovated and furnished. Eight faculty members from TUIT have undergone six months advanced training in IT at the C-DAC in Pune. Experts from C-DAC installed the equipment and conducted the training courses (MEA 2019).

Table: India- Uzbekistan bilateral Trade

Year	Imports from India (in US$ million)	Exports to India (in US$ million)	Total trade turnover (in US$ million)	Percentage Change over previous year
2007	64.0	9.5	73.5	23.73%
2008	79.9	11.1	91	23.80%
2009	101.6	23.1	124.7	37%
2010	123.8	27.2	151	21.10 %
2011	137.6	22.2	159.8	5.50%

(Source: Uzbekistan State Committee for Statistics)

According to the State Statistics Committee of Uzbekistan, India occupied the 15th place among countries that are trading partners of Uzbekistan, covering 0.7 per cent of the total trade turnover of the Uzbekistan.

India and Uzbekistan have highlighted absence of surface transport connectivity several times. Former Uzbekistan President during his visit to India in May 2011 again raised this issue and sought Indian support to several transport corridors being planned in Central Asia with Uzbek participation. There is considerable interest in Uzbekistan in cooperation with India in the area of information technology. Late President Karimov lauded India's achievements in this field in the Uzbek Parliament in 2001.

A number of Uzbek nationals are being imparted training in the field of Information Technology under ITEC programme. The India-Uzbekistan Centre for Information Technology, named after Jawaharlal Nehru, was inaugurated by Prime Minister during his visit to Uzbekistan in April 2006 in the Tashkent University of Information Technology (TUIT). An MoU (Memorandum of Understanding) on cooperation in the IT sector with Uzbekistan was signed during President Karimov's visit to India in May 2011 (MEA 2019).

MOS for Communication and IT Shri Sachin Pilot visited Tashkent from 13-15 October 2011 during which a Joint Action Plan (JAP) to upgrade the Jawaharlal Nehru Centre for IT was signed. Under the JAP Uzbekistan would also get GOI assistance in setting up a joint venture related to software development and production. India would upgrade the Jawaharlal Nehru Centre during the financial year 2012-13. Uzbek Air operates 15 flights a week between Uzbekistan and India. Under Inter-Governmental Agreements, Uzbek Airways has flying rights to Delhi, Amritsar and Trivandrum and Indian Airlines to Tashkent, Samarkand and Bukhara (Mushtaq 2012, 377).

India's Scope for Investment in Uzbekistan

The current level of economic cooperation between the two countries does fulfil the desired expectations especially when there is enormous scope of expanding this cooperation in different fields. One of them is textile industry in which Uzbekistan has tremendous export potential. Because of which the country focuses on the establishment of new facilities for advanced, high value added cotton, wool, and silk processing. Being the fourth largest cotton producer and the second largest cotton fibre exporter in the world with total annual cotton fibre production of 1.5 million tons, Uzbekistan has the broader agricultural base and is, as such, extremely interested in the development of export-oriented processing and manufacturing of food and agricultural products. Similarly, it is extremely rich in oil and gas and other mineral resources. For example, natural gas and coal reserves, combined together, are estimated at more than one trillion USD. Likewise, Uzbekistan has a well-developed industrial base that suits the construction and maintenance of aircraft. During the last few years, it supplied six IL-78 Mid-air Refueller planes to the Indian

Air Force, to be used in different international AF joint exercises, which were successfully displayed at the 'Aero-India' air show in Bangalore some years ago. Uzbekistan also has a well-developed industrial sector for the manufacturing and maintenance of broad range of construction materials including cement, bricks, tiles, and many more items. Uzbekistan holds leading position among Commonwealth of Independent States (CIS) in the production of finished and decorative stones like marble and granite exceed 85 million cubic meters, which suffices the country for the next century. In the like manner, Uzbekistan has a large scope for Indian investment in the chemical industry especially in the production/ processing of phosphorous, nitrogen fertilisers, cellulose, and paints and so on (Mushtaq & Bonday 2006, 315). Uzbekistan provides most favoured nation (MFN) status to 45 countries, including India. Friendly investment environment is based on a reliable legal frame and wide range of guarantees and benefits for investors, including tax incentives, providing land and buildings on attractive terms. Uzbekistan eyes to emerge as India's gateway to Central Asia (Economictimes.indiatimes.com, 2019).

Uzbekistan's Scope for investment in India

On the other hand, India has a rich potential and large pharmaceutical base. With her cooperation, Uzbekistan can develop its own export-oriented pharmaceutical industry. India's investment in this sector would undoubtedly bring considerable benefits to both the countries. Besides India's leadership in the development of information technologies is unmatched, and Uzbekistan needs to have collaboration with her in terms of introducing new data processing techniques into electronic management, banking and financial sectors. In fact, the work has already commenced more than a decade ago for the joint project seeking to set up Uzbek–Indian Information Technologies Centre in Tashkent. This will play a crucial role in strengthening the desired Indo-Uzbek ties at large. Uzbekistan can also share in the privatisation of and investment into large enterprises and banks with India. These bilateral ties can be extended for promoting cultural diplomacy keeping in view the fact that both Uzbekistan and India, have had intimate socio-cultural and trade relations from times immemorial. It is worth mentioning that both countries possess renowned historical sites and internationally developed transportation and communication systems that can be used to expand tourism at both places. Uzbekistan is quite suited to the realisation of these and many other projects for it has political and economic stability, high-skilled and inexpensive workforce, enormous deposits of natural resources, peculiar climatic conditions for agricultural development, economical energy resources, fairly developed rail, auto and air transport infrastructure, a well-developed legal system that provides strong guarantees, benefits, and advantages to foreign investors and large industrial base that can immediately be used for launching any kind of production with very little financial input or investment. This is besides number of facilities thrown open by the government for foreign investment into priority projects of the National Investment Program of Uzbekistan are exempted from income (profit) tax for the period of seven years. Similar facilities are available for launching projects in oil and gas, textiles, organic chemicals, transport and communication industries.

In other matters too, Uzbekistan offers ample scope for cooperation with India and other countries. The reason, besides other things, is that for the past several years the country has achieved macroeconomic stability. Its economy has grown at an average rate of about 4 per cent for almost a decade and it has emerged as one of the fastest growing and stable economies among CIS countries. In 2004-05, Uzbekistan's GDP rate reached to plus 7 per cent, the highest ever in its history. Due to favourable investment ambience and relaxed tax schemes, Uzbekistan attracted foreign investment worth 14 billion USD since 1991.

Notwithstanding these achievements, Uzbekistan has been facing problems that, to a certain extent, impede its overall economic development. These obstacles are primarily of geographical nature, and the most significant one of them is Uzbekistan's landlockedness. Like Liechtenstein, it is doubly landlocked; hence, it is too far from the major international transport communications which increases its dependence on transport infrastructure of the neighbouring countries. In this respect, diversification of transport communication systems is of crucial importance for Uzbekistan and its future economic prosperity. So far, the country has had access to international markets only through the routes situated to its North, North-West, and North-East. We hope that Uzbekistan's initiative to create international transport corridor through

Afghanistan to the sea ports of the India Ocean including Karachi and Mumbai, will soon materialise and break the country's dependence on existing transportation systems by connecting Uzbekistan and large Central Asian markets with India and the whole South Asian region. These are new transport corridors from Uzbekistan to Mazar-e-Sharif through Herat, Dogarun, Delaram or Milak in Afghanistan to the Persian Gulf sea ports of Chabahar, Bandar-e-Abbas and further on to Karachi in Pakistan and Ahmadabad and Mumbai in India (Mushtaq & Bonday 2006, 317).

Political Relations

Indo-Uzbek contacts were affable since early times. Relations between Central Asia and India have their extraction deep in history. The inhabitants of Indus Civilisation betrothed in cultural and trade relations with the areas lying in modern day Uzbekistan. The significant binding force between the two regions in the pre-Islamic period was Buddhism which penetrated Central Asia, inter alia, through areas of today's Uzbekistan. The founder of the Mughal dynasty, Zahirudin Mohammad Babur, came from Uzbekistan. Even during Soviet times, Indian leaders visited Tashkent. Prime Minister Jawaharlal Nehru accompanied by Indira Gandhi visited Uzbekistan in 1955 and 1961. Prime Minister Lal Bahadur Shastri journeyed Uzbekistan in January 1966 and died in Tashkent (MEA India, 2019). His name has been commemorated in Tashkent—a street and school is named after him and there is also a statue in his memory in the city. At the time when the coup d'état against Soviet leader Mikhail Gorbachev took place in August 1991 leading to the disintegration of the USSR, President Karimov in his capacity as Chairman of Supreme Soviet of Uzbekistan was visiting India. Uzbekistan declared its independence on 01.09.1991. Consulate General of India in Tashkent was formally inaugurated on 7 April 1987. Following Uzbekistan's independence, it was upgraded to the level of Embassy through the signing of a Protocol on Diplomatic and Consular matters on 18 March 1992 (MEA India, 2019).

The subsequent period has been characterised by frequent high-level exchanges. Prime Minister Narasimha Rao visited Uzbekistan in 1993 and Prime Minister Dr. Manmohan Singh on 25-26 April,2006. President

Karimov paid State visits to India in 1994, 2000, 2005 and of late in May 2011. The previous president of India Pranab Mukherjee formerly as Finance Minister visited Tashkent for the meeting of ADB (Asian Development Bank) Board of Governors in May 2010. On the sidelines, he held talks with Uzbek First Deputy PM (Prime Minister and Finance Minister Rustam S. Azimov and Prime Minister Shavkat Mirziyayev. EAM (External Affairs Minister) S.M. Krishna visited Tashkent in June 2010 to attend the SCO (Shangai Cooperation Organization) Summit. On the sidelines, he met President Islam Karimov. Earlier, EAM S. M. Krishna had visited Uzbekistan in October 2009. Minister of State for Information Technology, Sachin Pilot visited Tashkent in October 2011. In November 2011 COAS Gen. V. K. Singh visited Uzbekistan (Mushtaq 2012, 376).

Bilateral relations are managed through a robust mechanism including a Joint Commission, which oversees trade and economic relations. Uzbekistan and India have signed 74 Agreements/MOUs/ Protocols/Joint Statements in areas such as trade, investment, education, civil aviation, science and technology, telecommunications, agriculture and IT. Uzbekistan supported India's candidature for the non-permanent seat in the UN Security Council for 2011–12, and has been publicly supporting India's inclusion as permanent member of the UNSC. This was reiterated by President Karimov during his visit to New Delhi in May 2011. Uzbekistan supported India's candidature for the Executive Board of UNESCO (United Nations Educational, Scientific and Cultural Organization) in 2009. Uzbekistan voted for India for the Non-Permanent Membership of UNSC from the Asian Region for the 2011-2012 for which elections were held at the 6th Session of UNGA (United Nations General Assembly) in October 2010. The visit of the Uzbek Parliamentary Delegation led by the Speaker of the Olive Maglis (Uzbek Parliament), Erkin Kh. Khalilov, to India on 22-24 November 2005, also contributed immensely in strengthening the bilateral relations between the two countries. Both sides agreed to expand parliamentary and people-to-people contacts as one of the essentials for strengthening democratic institutions and trade and commercial ties.

Educational Cooperation

In the Pre-Soviet era, Indian students and researchers went to Central Asian institutes of higher studies and learning but now the flow is reversed. Earlier lot of people were moving to Soviet Central Asia for engineering, MBBS (Bachelor of Medicine), and many other courses for getting quality training and teaching in very high standard Russian maintained academies and institutes of higher learning. But in Post-Soviet Central Asia the trend reversed for lack of professional and trained teachers, equipment, and other resources in these now rapidly exhausting academies and institutes. Central Asian students are offered Government of India scholarships to come and study Information Technology, Management, English Language, Economics, Political Science and many other disciplines for which they lack facilities back at home. India also invited professionals from Central Asian countries and more especially from Uzbekistan to attend training programmes, workshops, seminars, symposia, conferences and field studies, etc (Gopal 2005, 176).

Six Uzbek educational institutions, nationwide, promote studies of Indian languages, particularly Hindi and Urdu, from primary to post-graduate level. An India Chair (Ambedkar Chair) was set up in 1996 at the University of World Economy and Diplomacy in Tashkent for the promotion of Indian Studies in Uzbekistan. Professor Azad Shamatov of the Institute of Oriental Languages, Tashkent has introduced Kashmiri language in the Institute initially in the form of a project. It is in fact the offshoot of an international conference titled 'Revival and Dynamics of Silk Route: Perspectives, Challenges and Opportunities' organised by the prestigious Centre of Central Asian Studies, University of Kashmir, in 2008 where the Professor after extensive deliberations promised to start research and teaching on Kashmiri language in Uzbekistan (Shamatov 2010).

Uzbekistan is a beneficiary of ITEC Programme since 1993–94. Currently 150 slots are being allotted annually. The ITEC Programme has been very well received in Uzbekistan. Areas of training include information technology, English for professionals, management, journalism, diplomacy, small business planning, remote sensing, banking and hotel management. ITEC slot utilisation from Uzbekistan has been close to 100 per cent during the last three years (in 2009-2011 100% slots utilised). Twenty Scholarships are being offered to Uzbekistan annually for various courses in Indian Universities under ICCR's Scholarship Programmes.

India is planning to establish Indian University of Central Asia in Kyrgyzstan which will be a very historical step for getting connected to Central Asia and promote the understanding of Indian culture there. But the experts suggest it would be better to set up this University in Uzbekistan for being the heart of Central Asia and located centrally in Central Asia. Uzbekistan is home to 136 ethnic groups and nationalities and houses all other nationalities of Central Asia in large numbers as compared to other republics and is geographically and economically most viable option to implement the idea of an Indian University of Central Asia. Furthermore, Uzbekistan is home to around 30 million people, approximately equal to the total population of all the other four Central Asian Republics. Tashkent can attract students and academia from other regions as well, i.e. Europe significantly, especially Eastern Europe, Middle East, Russia, West Asia, North-East Asia and South Asia, besides students of Greater Central Asian countries.

Socio-Cultural Relations

Historical accounts unveil incessant exchange of trips by Indian and Central Asians to each other's regions at least for the previous six centuries. Visitors came from a large spectrum: they included traders, scholars, artisans, artists, job-seekers, soldiers, adventurers, common men, etc. Indians travelling to Central Asia were adherents of faiths, such as Hinduism, Buddhism, Islam, Sikhism, Jainism, Zoroastrianism, etc., they hailed from different regions of the Indian subcontinent, though it is clear that the majority of Indian's visiting Central Asia belonged to the geographically contiguous area of the North-West, i.e. Kashmir and its adjoining areas of Ladakh, Baltistan, Chitral, etc., also the Punjab, the North-West Frontier provinces and Sindh (Gopal 2005, 1).

Lal Bahadur Shastri Centre for Indian Culture working under Indian Council for Cultural Relations (ICCR) was established in Tashkent in 1995 and has been a household name in Uzbekistan's cultural circles for its activities. Besides organising seminars relating to Indian culture, the

Centre also organises regular classes for Kathak, Yoga and Hindi language (ICCR India 2019). Uzbek Radio has completed 49 years of Hindi broadcasting in 2011. There is strong interest among Uzbeks in Indian films and music, and Indian movies dubbed in Uzbek are regularly telecast on local TV channels. It may be mentioned that after independence of Uzbekistan when radio programmes in all other foreign languages were stopped, only Hindi programmes could survive due to their popularity and are still popular. A Protocol on cooperation in the field of mass media was signed in October 1992. Subsequently, during the visit of Late President Islam Karimov to India in May 2000, another Protocol for cooperation in the field of information and mass media was signed. This Protocol envisaged cooperation involving exchange of TV programmes, visit of journalists, participation in international film festivals, cooperation among the filmmakers of both feature films and documentaries, visit of Radio and TV personnel, etc. During the same visit, an Agreement on Mutual Professional Cooperation between the National Information Agency of Uzbekistan and Press Trust of India was also signed. Uzbek and Indian artists regularly take part in a number of festivals and exhibitions organised in both the countries. Indian musicians and singers have been participating in the international music festival Sharq Taronalari held in Samarkand every year. Previously an Uzbek musical and dance troupe participated in the Surajkund Crafts Mela in Haryana, India (www.gov.uz/en/press/society 2019).

Between Central Asia and Kashmir

Like its desert climate of sweltering sun-drenched days and often frigid nights, Uzbekistan is a land of contrasts. It is a new nation with an old heart. Partially covered by the vast empty deserts of central Asia, the country's rich history and cultural legacy are evident in the beauty of its cities and the talents and resourcefulness of its people. These cities once connected east to west and Asia to Europe and acted as important centres of trade along the many routes that made up the commercial network known as the Silk Road. Today these urban centres still bear testimony to the nation's vibrant past. Taken over by the Russians in the early part of the 20th century, Uzbekistan only became a truly independent nation in the early 1990s. Although the nation's government is one of the worlds most repressive and its economy leaves many mired in poverty, the Uzbek people continue to display the same resilience that ensured their survival in a harsh desert land. Uzbekistan's cities of Samarkand once the capital of Timur's empire, Bukhara, and Khiva are a few of Central Asia's most historically significant cities.

Uzbekistan of the present times specially in relation to food habits, dressing pattern, language, art, religion, family, marriage, culture, etc., has similarities with Kashmir in India. Glimpses of Indian lifestyle are well experienced in almost all cities and towns, specially the most historical ones of Khiva, Samarkand and Bukhara and also one of the most fertile valleys of the world that is Fargana which is also the birth place of Zahiruddin Mohammad Babur (1483-1530) who laid down the foundation of Mughal Dynasty in India in 1526 AD.

Rural Life

Rural areas of Fergana, Andhijan, Namangan, Jizhak, Samarkand, Bukhara, Kashkadarya, etc., present that life in the country is a mixture of the modern and old fashioned. Four-lane highways are not used only by cars, trucks and buses but by donkey carts as well, though Tashkent is not witnessing it. Shepherds on horseback keep watch over their herds of goats and sheep. In the villages, the houses are built, as they always have been, with sun-baked bricks and mud mortar, a practice still common in rural Kashmir. Women are more likely to be field workers than men, often using just a garden hoe to work fields that stretch to the horizon. The farms are still likely to be enormous, a system of farming left over from the old days of the Soviet collectives.

Life in the Family

The structure of the Uzbek family reflects the country's Islamic culture. Elderly people are revered and respected, and men are considered superior to women exactly as in Kashmir. In the countryside and small towns, men and women do not eat at the same table. Especially when entertaining guests, women do not take part in the conversations of the men except in Tashkent and other modern and urbanised cities and towns which are more western, Russian and European in style and taste. When families have guests, the oldest man in the host family often says a prayer for the people gathered, expressing his hope for future cooperation and friendship. The oldest male guest then offers a prayer himself.

Weddings

Without a doubt, the most significant Uzbek event is a wedding and the last three months of the year (Oct., Nov. and Dec.) in Uzbekistan is the season of wedding ceremonies. Weddings are cause for much celebration in Uzbekistan just as in Kashmiri society. Ceremonies and practices often reflect a combination of ancient and modern influences. Traditionally, brides and grooms (known in Uzbek language as Mahren and Mahraz as in Kashmiri language) dressed in the same type of clothing their ancestors would have worn, with elaborate head dresses and jewellery for the women, and clothing embroidered with themes and colours unique to their family or tribe. Today the wedding couple is also equally likely to be dressed in western-style bridal clothes. The wedding ceremony and celebration follow the traditional pattern, though. An invitation might say the wedding starts at seven o'clock, but unlike western weddings, this does not mean the ceremony will occur then. At least two hours of music, feasting, and dancing precede the ceremony and even the arrival of the mahren and mahraz. Once they arrive, the ceremony begins, and the rest of the evening is given over to more feasting, music and dancing.

Non-verbal Communication

As in any culture, communication extends beyond the words people say. A glance or a gesture can convey more than words at times. The people greet one another which reveals much about how they feel. Men always greet one another with handshakes, even if they have not been formally introduced. They also shake women's hands, but often only if the woman extends her hand first. Friends and relatives of the same sex greet one another with kisses on the cheek, often several if they are very happy to meet. Women often greet one another with hugs. In Uzbekistan, and in other central Asian countries, like in Kashmir, the handshake exchanged between two men can be more than just a simple greeting. When men wish to show respect, they place their left hands over their hearts as they shake hands, and ever so slightly bow their heads. This gesture also shows gratitude, respect, or sorrow at parting. When a younger man makes his subtle bow to an older man, it is a sign of honour.

Festivals

To the Uzbek people, festivals are as much a state of mind as they are official holidays. Though there are many national holidays, village and town festivals, as well as weddings and birth parties, are often more lively and vibrant than some of the more somber state-sponsored occasions.

Novruz

In Uzbekistan March 21 is called Novruz, a word composed of two Uzbek words, nov, meaning 'new' and ruz, meaning 'day'. Unlike in the West, where New Year's Eve is celebrated with parties or lively social events, Novruz is a dynamic festival, spent with one's family close to home. The two-day festival of Novruz has been celebrated for at least 2, 500 years. It originated in Persia where kings wore a crown bedecked with symbols of rebirth and shared their riches with their people. Nomads moving into the Persian lands of central Asia adopted this rite of spring, following the course of the moon to set the dates of their celebrations as well their migrations and plantings. Though they did not refer to calendars, people knew this was the time when the days lengthened and warmed, and the growing season began again. Despite thousands of years of change and many foreign occupations, when March 21 comes Novruz is celebrated in much the same way.

Tajiks in Uzbekistan have stronger ties to Persia, and their Novruz meal reflects this particular influence. In Tajik families, the men and sons prepare the meal of shish kebabs and sweetened rice in hopes of sweetening the future. Elders bestow their blessings on children and give them gifts, making Novruz the favourite holiday for young people throughout the country. Novruz is a time for personal renewal as well. People prepare for the new year by cleaning their homes, buying and making new clothes, cancelling debts, and forgiving slights, and generally turning a new face to the future. They welcome the onset of the growing season but filling their homes with the fragrant branches of flowering fruit and nut trees, including almond, apricot, peach, and pomegranate. All these household preparations are completed before the morning star appears on March 21. The celebration of spring then continues over the next two weeks, as Uzbeks move outdoors for gatherings of family and friends.

Food

Uzbek cuisine reflects the influence of the nation's former status as a trading crossroad, with dishes and ingredients that come from both Asia and Europe. Daily dining is simple, incorporating foods that are in season. Daily dining is simple, incorporating foods that are in season. Breakfast is nourishing and quick: a yogurt drink and fruit. The main meal of the day is at noon. Rice, mutton, and non, a soft round bread that is torn into pieces, are the mainstays. The non is used to scoop up other bits of food. These basic dishes are in every cook's recipe book, often handed down from mother to daughter.

Fruits and Vegetables

In summer Uzbekistan's markets and kitchens are filled with fruits and vegetables grown in the fertile Fergana valley. Grapes, apricots, pears, apples, cherries, and citrus fruits find their way into markets for sale. Peaches from Uzbekistan once drew the interest of the Chinese and heightened their curiosity about their Uzbek neighbours to the west. The pomegranate with its brilliant red seeds is as important to the jewellery and embroidery designs of Uzbekistan as it is to the cooking. Traditionally, women dried summer fruits so they could have them for winter. Figs, apricots, raisins, and dates still add their sweetness to winter stews and deserts.

Meat and Spices

Meat is not plentiful in Uzbekistan. It is usually combined with rice and vegetables to make it go further. The fat-tailed Karakul sheep that provides the wool for rugs and other textiles is also the most commonly available meat and fat. Beef and horse-meat is substituted for mutton in most recipes. Two types of sausages are unique to the region, piyozli kazy and khassip, a sausage made of sheep's intestines and lungs. As a country that is at the crossroad of trade with the East, spices feature prominently in many dishes, especially cumin and pepper.

Tea

Tea, and the ceremonies that surround the making and drinking of it, are central to Uzbek life. Throughout the country, in cities and villages, men gather daily at the teahouse (chaykhana) to drink green tea and talk. The chaykhana is itself constructed according to regional traditions. It is built in the shade of a wooded area, often near a water source. The walls are open to catch the breezes; and patrons, traditionally only men, sit on low stools or recline on a low bed called a supa. People remove their shoes before entering the chaykhana and sit with their legs stretched out under the low table or curled beneath them on the supa. The guests sit where the host directs them. The farther they are seated from the door, the greater the honour bestowed on them.

In homes or chaykhanas, the tea ceremony is the same. The host pours tea three times into his cup, which is called a piala, each time pouring it back into the pot. This further steeps the tea leaves, making the tea more flavourful. Then he pours the brew for his guests, serving the one at a time. As each guest takes his piala from the host, they salute one another by placing their left hands on their hearts. The guest says rahmat, or 'thank you'. The pialas are filled only one-third full so the tea cools quickly. In a desert climate, this is done because of the heat.

Tea is central to the pace of Uzbek life. A hot climate does not reward those who hurry, so life proceeds in Uzbekistan at a leisurely pace. Tea helps set the pace, with its almost ritualised preparation. Brewing it, waiting for it to cool, and drinking it, all take time, and Uzbeks take many tea breaks. The common answer to a question about when something will happen is 'after tea'. It is not unusual for the answer to be 'tea after tea', which is clearly understood by all to mean, 'not in the very near future'. The chaykhana is also a place where there are no class divisions. Whether scientist or truck driver, janitor or doctor, when Uzbeks take tea together they show interest in and respect for one another with no regard for rank or status. Increasing unemployment has made the chaykhana the only destination for many men. They gather there to commiserate with those who are often facing similarly challenging economic realities.

Everyday Foods

If Uzbekistan had a national dish, it would surely be pilov, or pilaf, a rice-and-meat dish that has as many variations as there are cooks. Travellers through the centuries wrote of being welcomed into family homes or encampments and watching the women prepare the pilov in their honour. Often the cook would add quinces, currants, or raisins, giving the pilov a uniquely sweet taste. When all the water is absorbed, the pot would be emptied onto an enormous platter. Everyone would then gather around the platter, their right hands rolling the sticky rice around vegetables and pieces of meat. They would eat until all the food was finished.

Uzbeks have a tradition called morning pilov, when men gather between 6 and 7 a.m. Usually around 200 men are invited to these special gatherings to mark weddings, circumcisions, or deaths. They arrive dressed in sombre cloths; sit for a short time eating some pilov, and then leave, making room for the next wave of guests. Unlike other gatherings, no one drinks or makes toasts. Women do most of the cooking in Uzbekistan, but shashlik (known as kebab in Kashmir) is prepared by men like in Kashmir. Grilled on a metal stick, shashlik is usually made of mutton and served topped with onion. Shashlik is served in cafes as well as in homes.

Indian Community in Uzbekistan

The Indian community numbers 12,553 out of a total population of 07.18 million in Central Asia as of December 2018 (Uzbekistan- 382, Kazakhstan- 482, Kyrgyzstan- 1125, Tajikistan- 4814 and Turkmenistan- 5,750). It consists mainly of NRI students, entrepreneurs, traders, managers, representatives/employees of Indian or of multinational corporations, banks and hotels, and workers. The Indian community is well regarded, having a higher per capita income than the national averages and having adopted itself to local conditions. There are many NRIs employed by Indian companies and multinationals in Uzbekistan. It is felt that the Indian community in Central Asia has increased manifold over the years in view of the close economic and bilateral relations between the Central Asian countries and India and as such measures are being taken to promote linkages between India and its Diaspora (MEA, 2019). After having been a mainstay of the commercial scene in much of Central Asia, Southern Russia, Afghanistan, and Iran, the Indians disappeared from the historical scene because historians (both Western and Asian) ignored them. It was only in 1958 that the Russians (Antonova and Goldberg) put them back on the map. India needed horses, fresh and dried fruits, and nuts, which did not thrive well in India, whereas India produced cotton textiles, threads, dyes, and other textile related goods that Central Asia could not produce cost competitively (Scott 2002, 266). Past accounts unveil that for the last seven centuries there has been uninterrupted exchange of visits by Indians and Central Asians to each other's countries. Visitors came from a large gamut together with traders, scholars, artists, artisans, job seekers, soldiers, adventurers, travellers, common men, musicians, etc. Uzbek rulers actively supported both the trade and its traders. An undersized but vivacious Indian community resides in contemporary Uzbekistan. Indian Mission keeps up regular links with the community. The members of Indian community chip in gatherings prearranged on the occasion of Independence Day and Republic Day. The community graces with their presence other events like Eid, Novroz, Holi, Diwali and cultural programmes organised under the auspices of Lal Bahadur Shastri Centre for Indian Culture (Khan 2016, 04). In Samarkand and Bukhara many Indians have established business units over there in Indian items and goods and the response has remained stunning especially in pharmaceuticals, electronics, etc.

Conclusion

Ample opportunities of bringing India and Central Asia closer are beckoning for socio-economic and political grounds. National initiatives both in Uzbekistan and India are underway to strengthen the existing India-Uzbek relationship and new initiatives with strong cross-leveraging approach are sought out in vital connecting sectors. The age-old historical and cultural relations are getting new shape in the changing global world between Indian and Uzbekistan. Uzbekistan is making every effort to rebuild and restructure the lost connections and within that perspective both India and Uzbekistan have been working hard in areas of mutual interest. Educational institutions are being set up and cultural interactions as well as political exchanges are taking place to build this relationship. The development of India-Uzbekistan relations can also play significant role for stable, ordered and peaceful South and Central Asia since its geographic location makes it strategically important. Indo-

Uzbek economic ties need to be strengthened though finance can be an obstacle on Uzbek side which can affect trade between the two countries but Uzbekistan can surely offer goods in return to Indian goods under counter trade arrangements.

References

Doraiswamy, Rashmi (2017) Central Asia and South Asia: Economic, Developmental and Socio-Cultural Linkages. Delhi: Academy of International Studies, p. 5.

Dani, Ahmad Hassan (1996) Central Asia Today. Lahore Pakistan: Sang-e-Meel Publication, pp. 206, 191.

Chandra, Amiya (2015) India-Central Asia Relations: The Economic Dimension. Delhi: Pentagon Press.

Gopal, Surender (2005) Dialogue and Understanding-Central and India: The Soviet and Post-Soviet Era. New Delhi: Shipra Publications, pp. 1, 176.

Interview with Prof. Azad Shamatov, (Dec. 2010), Department of South Asian Languages, Institute of Oriental Languages, Tashkent, Uzbekistan.

Kaw, Mushtaq Ahmad (2010) Central Asia in Retrospect and Prospect. New Delhi: Readworthy, pp. 375, 376, 377.

Kaw, Mushtaq Ahmad, Bonday, Aijaz Ahmad (2006) Central Asia: Introspection. Centre of Central Asian Studies, University of Kashmir, pp. 315–19.

Khan, Nasir Raza (2016) Indian and Central Asia: Geopolitics, Economics and Culture. Delhi: Primus Books, p. 4.

Narayan, Rajiv, Tursonov Batir, Kumar Gaurav (2018) India - Uzbekistan Partnership in Regional Peace and Stability: Challenges and Prospects. Delhi: VIJ Books, pp. 10–15.

Scott C. Levi (2002) The Indian Diaspora in Central Asia and its Trade. Leiden: Brill, p. 266.

www.orfonline.org/research/india-central-asia-important-facilitate-north-south-trade-50442/. (access: 02.07.2019).

www.gov.uz/en/press/society. (access: 25.01.2019).

www.greaterkashmir.com/news/world/india-central-asian-nations-back-inclusive-afghan-peace- process/309460.html. (access: 14.01.2019).

www.iccrindia.net/tashkent. (access: 02.06.2019).

www.meaindia.nic.in/meaxpsite/foreignrelation/uzbekistan. (access: 05.05.2019).

www.mea.gov.in/images/attach/NRIs-and-PIOs_1.pdf. (access: 03.07.2019).

SIX

Khwaja Bakhtiyar Kaki of Osh (1173—1235) and the Indo-Kyrgyz Sufi-trajectory

Mohd. Sanaullah

Introduction

A trans-cultural trajectory of thought and culture never misses historicity in relation to the Indian subcontinent and Central Asia synchronising pluralism in unison. Indus Valley Civilisation, Vedas, Buddhism and Greco-Buddhism, the Mauryans, Bactria, Transoxiana, Zoroastrianism, Islam, Sufism, Abbasid-Turkic and Mongol culture, etc (Cunningham: 1877, Dhammika: 1993, Saliba: 1955, Sanaullah: 1990, 2008a, 2007, 2016) are the focal points of reference in such an odyssey that combines certain areas of Indology, Iranology, Turkology, Mongolian Studies, Eurabia and Islam (Sanaullah:2003, 2006). Since antiquity, geographical, religious, spiritual, cultural, political and literary amalgamation between Transoxiana, India, Persia and Arabia has never been short of any historical references as testified by original Arabic, Persian and Turkic sources (Ibn Al-Athir: 1965, Al-Nasafi: 1999, Bukhara'i: 1377 AH, Kashghari: 1897, Dughlat: 1898, Al-Hamadani: MS Edinburgh, Jujani: 1873, Al-Naqshbandi: 2010, Sanaullah: 2008a, 2013), besides numerous studies in European languages. Such a cross-cultural rendezvous connecting India, Central Asia and Arabia constitutes a legacy of paramount significance in Sufism, especially in its pantheist schools that are contextualised in terms of historicity with perennial philosophies of India, in those of Vedas, Upanishads, Buddhism and Shamanism in particular (Elverskog: 2010) that stand as common thread in the Ibn-Arabi-Hallajian pantheist Sufi traditions of Murcia, Cairo, Aleppo, Baghdad, Isfahan, Samarqand, Osh and Delhi. Osh has been a centre of Hallajian pantheism as shown by Massignon (Massignon: 1941-46a, 1982, Sidikov: 1946, 77–8, Schimmel: 1975, Sultanova: 2011) and so is Delhi in India (Schimmel: 1978) in the personae of Sarmad (1590-1661) on footsteps of Ain Al-Qudat Hamdani (d. 1131) and Qadi Hamiduddin Nagauri of Lawā'ih fame (Dabistan-e-Mazahib: 1843, Cook: 2007, Ernst: 1985, Sanaullah: 2010). It may be noted that Mansur Al-Hallaj (858–922) uttering ana al-haq (Halaj: 1913) well-coordinates with the Upanishadic mahavakyas Aham Brahmasmi and Tat Tvam Asi (Raphael: 1992). This is another thread in the tapestry of Indo-Central Asian relations over the ages.

Migrations and Sufism: The Central Asian connections

A wide array of sources (annals, chronicles, Sufi-malfūzāt, etc.) from the early 13th century onwards have documented the arrival of Muslims and establishment of the Delhi Sultanate (1206-1526). Qutbuddin Aibak (r. 1206–10), a slave of Shihabuddin Muhammad Ghauri (1173–1202 and 1202–06) captured Delhi circa 1193 defeating the Rajput armada without much resistance. This marked the beginning of Muslim rule in India. Aibak constructed Quwwatul Islam mosque with a 72.50-meter-high minaret known as Qutb Minar epitomising Delhi as stronghold of Islam without resorting to massacre of the populace or demographic dislocation. The successive years witnessed a series of monuments in Dar Al-Khilafa such as tombs of Sultan Shamsuddin Iltutmish (r. 1211–36) and Imam Zamin (the Turkish Imam of Quwwatul Islam Mosque during the rule of Sikander Lodhi, r. 1489–1517, and the additions by Sultan Alauddin Khalji [r. 1296-1316]: Alai Darwaza, Alai Madrasa and Alai Minar) that defied time as hallmarks of emerging Delhi Sultanates' much envied architecture (Khan: 2000: 166–7, Beg: 1982, Troll: 2004, Stepen Carr: 1979, Frykenberg: 1986, SGP: 1916, Ataullah: 1982). Iltutmish reproached non-Muslim citizens resisting demands of the theologians to confront them with death or conversion to Islam (Barani: 1972). Qutbuddin Aybak's rule coincided with the election of Genghis Khan as the great leader of the Mongol hordes. As elaborated by Juzjani (1873: vol I, pp. 508–51), the sack of major Muslim cities like Bukhara, Isfahan and Baghdad and the subsequent large-scale devastation in Central and West Asia in the next 50 years led to migration of peoples from all wakes of life, including the nobles, scholars, Sufi saints and men of letters, to Delhi, hence the epithet Hadrat-e-Dehli, where Caliph was mentioned in Friday sermons and on coins, in a pluralist culture of multi-religious complexity. The Sufi hospices and shrines augmented the pluralistic fabric of the city as evident in the famous saying of Shaykh Nizamuddin Auliya (1238–1325) disapproving conversion.

Central Asia, especially Kyrgyz Republic, stands central to the Sufi-trajectory of the Indian subcontinent, as Chishtiya and Naqshbandiya orders in their early stages are linked to Farghana valley. The Chishtiya is the oldest Mystic order to get introduced in India on the hands of Khwaja Moinuddin Chishti Ajmeri (1142–1236). Khwaja Qutbuddin Bakhtiar Oshi Kaki (1173–1235) originally belonged to Osh, presently in Kyrgyzstan, succeeded Khwaja Chishti, and was a spiritual master of Baba Farid Ganj-e-Shakar (1172–1265). Successive Sufi masters such as Qazi Hamiduddin Nagauri (d. 1279) and Shaykh Nizamuddin Auliya (1238–1324), Shaykh Nasiruddin Avadhi Chiragh-e-Dehli (d.1356), Shaykh Maulana Burhanuddin Gharib (d. 1340), Shaykh Saleem Chishti (d.1572), Makhdum Alauddin Ali Ahmad Sabir Kaliyri (AH 592-684), Haji Imdadullah Muhajir Makki (d. 1899) and his disciples in the Deobandi School, including Mohammad Qasim Nanautvi (d. 1878), Mahmudul Hasan (d. 1920), Rashid Ahmad Gangohi (d. 1905), Mohammad Ilyas Kandhlawi (d. 1944) and Husain Ahmad Madani (d. 1957), etc., popularised it in the length and breadth of the subcontinent. the most eminent Sufi masters of the order in India (Sanaullah, 2008b, 337–66).

The Suhrawardiya silsila founded by Shaykh Shihabuddin Suhrawardi (1144–1234) was next to the Chishtiya order in India. Prominent Indian Suhrawardis include Shaykh Bahauddin Zakaria Multani (1170–1262), Syed Jalaluddin Surkh Bukhari (1199–1291), Makhdum Jahanian Jahangasht (d. 1384), among others (Suvorova: 2004) who had strong Central Asian connections.

Medieval and modern studies have shown strong historical Sufi Naqshbandi links between the Indian sub-continent and Central Asia

(Artman: 2016, Weismann: 2007, Algar: 1998, Kabbani: 1995, Sanaullah: 2013). The order was founded by Khwaja Ahmad Ata Yasawi (d. 1166), but it was Khwaja Bahauddin Naqshband (d. 1389) who popularised it among the Turks and Mongols of Central Asia and Transoxiania (Kashghari: 1897, Eden: 2018). Khwaja Baqi Bi-Allah (1563–1603) came to India from Kabul during Akbar's reign in the later part of 16th century and popularised the order. The Mughals had great respect and attachment to the Naqshbandi saints. Shaykh Ahmad Yassavi's mausoleum was built by Emir Timur (Timer-lane) who paid respectful visits to his shrine (Sanaullah: 2008a). He also treated Khwaja Bahauddin Naqshband with profound respect. Babur was deeply attached to Khwaja Muhammad Qadi, a successor of Khwaja Ubaid Allah Ahrar (Badi'a: 2010). Descendents of Khwaja Ahrar had come to India after its conquest by Babur. When Khwaja Khan Mahmud, a descendent of Khwaja Ahrar came to India, he was received by Humayun with great honour. Akbar accorded a welcome to Khwaja Shahid. Khwaja Baqi Bi-Allah (1563–1603) established a Sufi-center in Delhi and devoted all his time to the spiritual and moral training of the people. Later on, two extraordinary disciples of Khwaja Baqi Bi-Allah, namely Shaykh Ahmad Sirhindi and Shaykh Abd al-Haq Muhaddith Dehlawi, popularised the order in India, Arabia and Turkey.

Khwaja Qutbuddin Bakhtiyar Kaki of Osh (1173–1235)

Khwaja Qutbuddin Bakhtiyar Oshi Kaki is associated with several honourifics such as Qutub-ul-Aqtaab, Qutub-ul-Islam, Malik-ul-MaShaykh, Sultan-ul-Tariqat, Burhan-ul-Haqiqat, Rais-us-Salikin, Imam-ul-Aamileen, Siraj-ul-Aulia, Taj-ul-Asfia, etc. As stated by a number of medieval Persian Sufi sources (Amir Khurd: 1302 AH), Jamali: 2015, Sijzi: 1302 AH), he was born in the progeny of Imam Jafar Sadiq in Osh (Fergana Valley) in the Hijri Year of 582 / 1173 AD. Abul Fazl ibn Mubarak noted (1873–1907:363) that Kaki's father Syed Kamaluddin ibn Syed Musa died leaving him a boy of one and a half years. The genealogical line ascends to Prophet Muhammad via Syed Kamaluddin, son of Syed Musa, son of Syed Ahmed Awashi, son of Syed Kamaluddin, son of Syed Mohammed, son of Syed Ahmed, son of Syed Raziuddin, son of Syed Husamuddin, son of Syed Rashiduddin, son of Syed Jafar, son of Nafi-ul-Wajood, son of Syed Ali Musa Raza, son of Syed Musa Kazim, son of

Jafar Sadiq, son of Mohammed Baqar, son of Syed Zain-ul-Abideen, son of Imam Husain. Khwaja Abu Hafs Oshi was his earliest teacher when he was 5 years old. In Baghdad, he met Khawaja Moinuddin Chishti in Masjid Imam Abu Al-Lais Al-Samarqandi and became his disciple and at the age of 17 years was appointed khalifa (successor) for Delhi.

Khwaja Kaki has himself mentioned (Kaki: 1310) that he arrived in Delhi via Ghazni and Multan. Delhi was under Sultan Shamsuddin Iltutmish (reign 1211–1236), the third ruler of the slave dynasty of Turkic origin after Qutbuddin Aibak (reign 1206–10) and Aram Shah (reign 1210–11). He stayed in Kilokhari or Shahr-i-Nau, the most happening place for roughly the whole of the 13th century, before moving to Mehrauli or the old part of Delhi which was soon overpopulated with large numbers of emigrants from Central Asia and Iran fleeing the Mongol carnage. The adjoining Ghiyaspur that saw hospice and mausoleum of Shaykh Nizamuddin Auliya, besides tomb of Humayun later on, became centre of spiritual activities and Sufi initiations frequented by princes, intellectuals, poets and singers who came in search of peace and tranquility (Barani: 1862, fols. 60b; 73b–77b). According to Khusrau in Qiran us sa'dain (N.D.a: 41), the bohemian Sultan Moizuddin Qaiqabad (r. 1287-1290) built Qasr e Moizzi in Kilokhari, after moving his capital from the crowded old city. It was while relaxing here that Sultan Ruknuddin Firuz (r. 30 April 1236-20 November 1236) learnt of the coup by Raziya Sultan (r. 1236-1240). He was captured by Raziya's forces from here and was imprisoned before his unceremonious elimination (Juzjani: 1881: I, 636). Iltutmish venerated dervishes, so he went out of the city to welcome Khwaja Kaki and requested him to stay in the seat of power, but the latter preferred to stay at Kilokhari. The Sultan, however, used to attend Khwaja Kaki's congregation twice a week in order to receive his spiritual blessings and guidance, and later on became a regular and most dutiful disciple. At this stage, he requested him to come and stay with him in the city as attending him at Kilokhari which he must do, warranted much of his time which he could save to attend to the affairs of his government; hence the Khwaja agreed and shifted to the mosque of Malik Ainuddin in the city.

Khwaja Kaki was Kaki was assigned the wilayat of Delhi by his spiritual guide Khwaja Moinuddin Chishti. The Concept of wilayat in Sufism holds especial position. Sufis like Shaykh Yahya Maneri (1263-

1381) in his Maktoobat (1315 AH, p. 24 et seq) and Ashraf Jahangir Simnani (1285-1386) in Maktoobat e Ashrafi (MS: Letter No. 73) and Abdul Ghafur Danapuri (1307 AH) have chiefly elaborated the theme. It was a territorial distribution on spiritual lines of guidance and protection, parallel to the political authority enjoyed by the Sultans.

Sufis and the Sultans: Kaki and Iltutmish (r. 1211–36).

The relation of Sufis with the Sultans has been a significant point of reference to the power-equation especially during Delhi Sultanate in India. The Sultans venerated the Sufi masters, along side the scholars, and patronised them. Their veneration and patronage stemmed from the spiritual powers enjoyed by the Sufis aside the genealogical sacredness as they usually hailed from the Prophetic lineage. Sultan Al-Hind Khwaja Moinuddin Chishti's arrival to India coincided with the conquest by the Turks. As per Sufi accounts, Moinuddin Chishti had prophesied Shihabuddin Ghauri's victory in the second battle of Tarain in 1192 in which the Chauhan ruler Rai Pithaura or Prithviraja, who harassed the Khwaja and his disciples in Ajmer, was defeated. The Khwaja and his khalifa for Delhi Khwaja Bakhtiyar Kaki were held in high esteem by Sultan Shamsuddin Iltutmish (ruled 1211–36). The Sufis, specially the Chistis, in order to maintain their visible independence, tried to alienate themselves from the state system. But while, doing so, they still provided tacit support to the activities of the state in a covert manner (Digby: 1984, 1986, 1990, Habib: 1981, Nurul Hasan: 2008, Pinto: 1995, Rizwi: 1975, Kumar: 2007, 2010).

Iltutmish requested Khwaja Kaki to accept the powerful post of Shaykh Al-Islam, but Kaki politely turned down the offer. During Delhi Sultanate, only a Danishmand was to be appointed as Sadr-e-Jahan or Sadr al-Sudur, Shaykh Al-Islam, Qazi, Mufti, Muhtasib, Imam, Khatib or a teacher in a seminary supported by the government. (Qalander: n.d., p. 212, Sijzi: 1302, p 237, Nizami: 1961, p. 158) Qazi al-Mamalik was the highest judicial authority after the Sultan who consulted him while appointing qazis for different cities of the country. Usually, Sadr e Jahan and Qazi al-Mamalik was the same person, as seen in the person of Minahj Siraj, the author of Tabaqat e Nasiri, who is known as Sadr e Jahan (Jujani: 1873, p. 219, Barani: 1862, p. 126). The office of the Shaykh al-Islam managed all the ecclesiastical affairs of the state, though in some cases it was an honorary title conferred by the Sultan. Sijzi (1302, p. 24) condemns those who aspire to get such a title. Shaykh Bahauddin Naqshband was given such honorific title by Iltutmish (Jamali: 1311 p. 169). Scholars such as Syed Nuruddin Mubarak Ghaznawi, Shaykh Jamaluddin Bistami, Maulana Najmuddin Sughra, Syed Qutbuddin (during the reign of Bahram Shah) and Shaykh Rafi'uddin had held the post (Dehlawi: 1309, p. 28, Amir Khurd: 1302, p. 54, Juzjani: 1873, p. 196). Shaykh Jamaluddin Bistami was assigned the office by Iltutmish after Khwaja Kaki declined to accept it (Sijzi: 1302, p. 4). There are evidences to show that the Sufis participated and prayed during the warfare. They also advised the Sultans on the methodology of expedition on warfare. For instance, when Sultan Hussain (1458–79) of Jaunpur came to invade Delhi and laid siege to it, Bahlul Lodi (r.1451–89) stood bare headed and prayed at the tomb of Bakhtiyar Kaki throughout the night. It is said that he received a staff from a heavenly person in the morning and then attacked the enemy successfully, as a result of which Sultan Hussain's army was defeated and forced to retreat to Jaunpur.

The state patronage of the Sufis during Delhi Sultanate witnessed some rivalries between them and mediated to diffuse the situation. One of the examples is associated to Khwaja Kaki whose public popularity and position as venerated by the Sultan antagonised Shaykhul Islam Najmuddin Sughra, a Sufi of his own order. Najmuddin and Bakhtiyar Kaki's spiritual guide Khwaja Moinuddin Chishti were disciples of the same sheikh, Khwaja Usman Harwani. The Shaykh Al-Islam was not taking kindly to the growing popularity of Kaki and his influence in political circles. Iltutmish himself was a devotee and, according to a later tradition, had become a khalifa or spiritual successor of the sheikh. Seeking to prevent the tensions between Najmuddin and Bakhtiyar Kaki from escalating, Moinuddin Chishti, who was on a visit to Delhi, asked his disciple to leave the place and accompany him to Ajmer (Sijzi: 1302, p.64). The news of the departure of the saints was perceived as a sign of calamity by the Sultan and the people. They followed the Sufi-masters for miles, crying and wailing. Touched by the grief of the ruler and the ruled alike, Moinuddin Christi allowed Bakhtiyar Kaki to remain in Delhi (Sijzi: 1302, p. 65). As a patron saint of the city, Kaki enjoyed prestige and authority, and influenced the Sultan's style of governance. Sometimes, the Sultans also engaged the Sufis in matrimonial alliance, possibly to obtain their moral and spiritual support and to elevate themselves. Baba Farid, it is said, married Sultan Balban's daughter. Mohammad bin Tughlaq (r. 1325-1351) had married his daughter, Bibi Rasti to Shaykh Fathullah and the latter stayed with the Sultan for some times, but quite hesitantly. However, when the Sultan knew about his discomfort, he allowed him to go back home. Similarly, Shaykh Sadr al-Din, the son of Shaykh Baha al-Din had married the grand daughter of Iltutmish. In the down south, Shaykh Nuru'llah (d.1430-31A.D.), a Qadiriya Shi'i Sufi, had married the daughter of Bahmani Sultan Shihab al-Din Ahmed I (1422-36A.D.). Bahlul Lodi had also married his daughter to Shah Abdullah Qureshi, who was a majzub and descendant of Shaykh Baha al-Din Zakaria Multani (1170-1262) and was a saintly person. He became Shaykh-ul-Islam of Delhi during Sikandar Lodi (r.1489-1517). The young son of Abdullah, Shaykh Hasan, had become an important disciple of Shaykh Burhanuddin Gharib Chishti (d. 1344) of Kalpi.

The construction of Hauz-e-Shamsi (water reservoir for the city-dwellers built in 1230), Gandhak ki baoli (step-well) for the Khwaja along with naming of Qutb-Minar is associated with such veneration of Khwaja Kaki (Smith: 2005). The Hauz-e-Shamsi and its adjacent Auliya Masjid, Jahaz Mahal and the picturesque spring garden had become a rendezvous of the spiritual and intellectual elite of the city. Much to the chagrin of the puritanical ulama, music assemblies (mahfil-i-sama or Sufi music) were frequently organised. The institution of sama was legalised in Delhi owing to efforts by Qazi Minhaj Siraj when he was qazi of Delhi (Amir Khurd: 1302, p. 239, Dehlawi: 1309, p. 79). Khwaja Kaki was the moving spirit behind them. Sources record (Lakhnawi: 1999, vol.i, p. 115, Jamali: 1311, Amir Khurd: 1302) that Khwaja Kaki held sama-sessions in his own hospice. Sometimes, he joined them at the residence of Qazi Hamiduddin Nagauri or at other Sufi hospices in the city. For him, the music was the enchantment of love; the secret of divine love as love was the divine secret: Sarod cheest ke chandeen fasoon-e-ishq daroast, Sarod mehram-e-ishq ast-o-ishq mehram-e-oast. When the qawwal sung Ali Sajistani's couplet: Kushtagaan-e-khanjar-e-tasleem raa, Har zamaan azz gheb jaan-e-deegar ast (For the victims of the sword of divine love, there is a new life every moment from the unseen), ecstasy gripped the Khwaja who fell unconscious. He remained in the state of ecstasy for three days and breathed his last on the fourth day. At the time of death, Kaki's head was resting on the thigh of Qazi Hamiduddin Nagauri, while both of his hands were in the lap of Sheikh Badruddin Ghuznavi (Lakhnawi: 1999, vol. I, pp. 114–15). Khwaja Abu Said Tabrezi, a khalifa of Khwaja Kaki, said that the Khwaja has willed that only that person may lead his funeral prayer who never committed sexual sins in his life. Sultan Shamsuddin Iltutmish led the prayer, saying that the Khwaja had willed to expose him on a secret never divulged by him to anyone before (p. 174). He died in 633 AH/1235 AD and was buried in Mehrauli in a non-cemented grave. Some constructions came up since 948 AH.

Personal accounts

A picture of renouncement, patience and forbearance, Khwaja Qutbuddin Bakhtiyar Kaki and his family (he had married twice) lived an austere life. He refused to accept state favours and lived on futooh (un-asked offerings), often facing unavoidable starvation for days. His wife would buy some provisions through a loan from the wife of a neighbouring provision dealer. Once the lender taunted Khwaja's wife by saying that if she stopped lending, the borrower and her children would starve to death. When this taunt was brought to the notice of the Khwaja, he forbade his wife to borrow anything from the neighbour in future but to take out as many kaks (a kind of very tasty bread) as she needed from the niche of his hujra (cell) by reciting Bismillah. The lady did the same and the necessity of a loan never arose again. It was this miraculous incident which indicates the popular suffix of the word of 'Kaki' to Khwaja's name. The self-imposed extreme poverty of the Khwaja, however, never stood as a hurdle to be magnanimous as per Sufi traditions. Whatever futooh came to his hospice were quickly distributed among the poor and the needy every day. If nothing was left in the kitchen, he would order his attendants and disciples to start distribution of plain water as a humble token of his hospitality to all callers.

Khwaja Kaki was ever ready to help the visitors, with whatever he had in terms of food, clothing, money or recommendation to the Sultan. Once, Nasiri, a poet came to Delhi from Transoxiana to his hospice and asked him for a favour of prayer to the effect that Sultan Iltutmish rewarded him generously for a panegyric ode in his praise. Khwaja Kaki prayed for him. Nasiri obtained an audience at the court and the Sultan gave him one thousand tankas for each of the couplet of his qasidah, which comprised thirty-five couplets. Nasiri brought that amount to the Khwaja and offered half of that to him for distribution among the poor, but the Khwaja did not accept the offer.

Works and Legacy

Khwaja Kaki's works include a Diwan (1879), Dalil Al-Arifeen (n.d. : Lucknow: Matb' Hafiz Mahmud), Mathnawi e Mai Rang (1890: MSS: Sprenger 453, Rieu Suppt. 238) and Fawaid Al-Salekeen (n.d.: Matba Mujtaba'i: MSS: Bankipur xvii 1640, Ivanov Curson 413). Dalil al-Arifeen is a collection of the conversations of Khwaja Moinuddin Chishti compiled by his disciple Hamiduddin Nagauri (d. 1279), while in Fawaid al-Salikeen Khwaja Kaki collected utterances of his mentor Khwaja Moinuddin Chishti (Agha Buzurg: 1983, vol. 9, pp. 127, 883; Dehlawi: 1309, p. 38).

Khwaja Kaki had nominated Sheikh Fariduddin Ganj-i-Shakar as his spiritual successor. Also known as Baba Farid and especially venerated in Sikh tradition (for his devotional poetry incorporated in the Guru Granth Saheb), the sheikh, called a mad boy (diwana bachcha) in younger days, had met Bakhtiyar Kaki at his native Multan and joined the order as his disciple. It is at Ajodhan that Farid's reputation as a charismatic spiritual leader was built, which made him something of a living legend (Aquil, 2003b; Eaton, 2003; Nizami: 1955). Significantly, as an all-powerful noble under Nasiruddin Mahmud (r. 1246–66), Ghiyasuddin Balban (1266–87), then known as Ulugh Khan, was a devotee of Baba Farid (Sijzi: 1302, pp. 89–90). Ali Asghar, himself a descendant of the sheikh, recorded in his early 17th-century text that the saint had married Ulugh Khan's daughter Bibi Huzaira and had six sons and three daughters from her (Chishti: 1301, 215–8; Lahori: n.d.p.301). The saint's favourite son, Nizamuddin (not to be confused with his spiritual successor Nizamuddin Auliya) had joined Ghiyasuddin Balban's army. He is said to have died fighting the Mongol invaders in Punjab (Sijzi: 1302, pp. 100, 200). Some sources have given names of 22 khalifas succeeding the Khwaja, including the most prominent three namely Baba Farid Ganj e Shakar, Badruddin Ghaznawi and Shah Khizr Qalander Rawi who actively spread the order (Sijzi: 1302, p. 176).

Ibn Battuta (1304–69) arrived in Delhi during the reign of Mohammad Tughlaq (r. 1325–51) and was appointed Qadi of the Malikiya School of jurisprudence by the later. He was also given charge of Kaki's mausoleum, with a budget of fifty-thousand tankas and an anticipatory crop of hundred thousand maunds of wheat and rice (Ibn Battutta: 2012, pp. 210-211) Ibn Battuta has given account of public kitchen attached to the mausoleum.

Conclusion

Muslim theology, culture and politics of medieval India owe much to Fergana valley in the very process of genesis and development. Delhi Sultanate (1206–1526) and Mughal Empire (1526–1857) are related to Central Asia as nobility, armada, aristocracy, academia, art, music and literature of the regions represent dimensions of interactions and exchanges through ages. Babur as founder of Mughal dynasty, Burhanudddin Ali Farghani Murghinani (1135–97), the celebrated author of Hidaya as central to Hanafi jurisprudence, Hazrat Shah Jalal (1271-1346) as khalifa of Shaykh Ahmad Yassawi (1093–1161) via Shaykh Ahmad Kabir Suhrawardi (1119-1182 and Shaykh Jalaluddin Surkh Posh Bukhari (1198–1292) in India (Haider: MS Sylhet, Khusrau: N.D.b, Sanaullah:2013), Khwaja Bahauddin Naqshband (1318–89) as founder Naqshbandi seer, Khwaja Qutbuddin Bakhtiyar Kaki (1173–1235) as chief khalifa of Khwaja Moinuddin Chishti (1141–1236) to spread Chishtiya order in India, among others, stand as central historical references in the trajectory. The pantheist humanism Chishtis and Suhrawardis surpassing Khawajegan-martyrology (Cook: 2007, Eden: 2018, Ernst: 1982), Gross and Urunbaev: 2002) and incorporating elements of Upnishadic spirituality (Sanaullah: 2007, 2008a, 2009, 2015) and Hikmat Al-Ishrāq (Sanaullah: 1999) gains greater relevance in contemporary parlances of fraternity, co-existence and peace in our times.

Kaki's succession as link between Moinuddin Chishti and Baba Farid Ganje-e-Shakar (1172-1265) and works both in poetry and prose given above posit him as divine par excellence among his contemporaries as well as for the posterity reserving vast accounts of veneration in all major historical and Sufi compendiums of the Indian subcontinent in Arabic, Persian, Urdu, English and French languages. The accounts given in sources like M'ārij al-Wilāyat, Mir'āt Al-Asrār, Gulzār e Abrār, Sawāti' Al-Anāar, Riyad Al-Arifeen, Akhbar Al-Akhyar, Siyar Al-Auliya, Khair Al-Majalis, Siyar Al-Arifeen, Siyar Al-Aqtāb, Siyar Al-Auliya, Tārikh e Ferishta, Raudatul Aqtāb, Haft Iqlīm, Makhzan Al-Ghrā'ib, Rehla Ibn Battuta, Nuzhat Al-Khwātir, Sham' e Anjuman, etc, besides Beale's Oriental Biographical Dictionary, Garcin de Tassy's Mémoire sur les particularités de la religion musulmane dans l'Inde, among numerous other books, provide the researcher with new avenues of investigation. Infused with tremendous historical, academic and social retrospective dimensions to be investigated in perspectives of historiography, the Indo-Kyrgyz Sufi trajectory augments itself in the person, passion and travails of Khwaja Kaki and proposes perspectives of research in terms of historiography surpassing hagiography or martyrology.

References

Abul Fazl (1873-1907). Ain-e-Akbari. English translation by Heinrich Blochmann and Colonel Henry Sullivan Jarret, 1973-1907. The Asiatic Society of Bengal, Calcutta. Vol III, Saints of India.

Agha Buzurg, Tehrani (1983). Al-Dari'a ila tasanif al-Shia. Beirut: Dar Al-Adwa. Vol 9. 3rd edition.

Al-Aal, Badi'a Mohammad Abd (2010). Al-Naqshbandiya: Nash'atuha wa tatawwuruha lada al-Turk. Cairo: Dar Al-Thaqafa Li Al-Nashr.

Algar, Hamid (1998). Sufism: Principles and Practice. Islamic Publications International.

Al-Hamadani, Rashid Uddin Fadlullah (1912). Jami al-Tawarikh: MS Edinburgh. Edited and annotated by Blochet, 15.

Al-Naqshbandi, Abdul Majeed (2010). Al-Hadaiq Al-Wardiya fi Ajillai al-Sada al-Naqshbandiya: DKi, Beirut.

Al-Nasafi, Najmuddin (1999). Al-Qand fi zikr ulama Samarqand. Tehran: Markaz Nashr al-Turath al-Makhtut.

Amir Khurd, Syed Mohammad ibn Mubarak Kirmani (1302). Siyar Al-Auliya. Delhi: Muhibb e Hind Press.

Anna Sovorova (2004). Muslim Saints of South Asia. Rutledge Curzon.

Artman, Vincent Michael (2016). The State and the Sacred: Memory, Theology and Identity in Kyrgstan (PhD thesis)

Ataullah, PhD thesis (2008): The City of Delhi during the eighteenth century: A Socio-Cultural Profile. Centre of Advanced History, Department of History, Aligarh Muslim University.

Beale, Thomas William (1881). The Oriental Biographical Dictionary. Calcutta: The Asiatic Society under the

superintendence of Henry George Keen.

Barani, Ziauddin (1972). Fatawa-i-Jahandari. Lahore: University of the Punjab.

Barani, Ziauddin (1862). Tarikh Firoz Shahi. Edited by Sir Syed Ahmad Khan. Bib. Indica. Calcutta.

Barthold, W (1928). Turkestan Down to the Mongol Invasion. London: Lusac.

Beg, Sangin (1982). Sairul Manazil, ed. Sharif Husain Qasmi. Delhi:Ghalib Institute.

Bilgirami, Ghulam Ali Azad (1910). Maa'thir al-Kiram. Agra:Matba' Mufid 'Ām.

Bukhara'i, Mirza Shams (1377). Tarikh Bukhara, Khoqand wo Kashghar: Tehran: Markaz Paruhasti Miras e Maktoob.

Chishti, Abdurrahman (MS) Mirat al-Asrar. MSS: Maulana Azad Library, Aligarh Muslim University.

Chishti, Ali Asghar (1301). Jawahir e Faridi. Lahore: Karimi Press.

Chishti, Allah Diya (1913). Siyar Al-Aqtab. Navalkishore Press.

Cook, D (2007). Martyrdom in Islam (Cambridge) ISBN 9780521850407.

Cunningham, Alexander (1877). Inscriptions of Asoka. Calcutta: Office of the Superintendent of Government Printing.

Dabistan-e-Mazahib (1843), translated by David Shea and Anthony Troyer. Oriental Translation Fund, Paris.

Danapuri, Abdul Ghafur (1307). Nus'h al-ibad fi wojood al-qutub wa al-abdal. Lucknow. Nami Press.

Dehlawi, Abdul Haq Muhaddith (1309). Akhbar Al-Akhyar fi Asrar Al-Abrar. Delhi: Matba' Mujtaba'i.

de Tassy, Garcin (1869). Mémoire sur les particularités de la religion musulmane dans l'Inde. 2nd edition. Paris: Adolphe Labite.

Dhammika, Shravasti (1993). The Edicts of King Ashoka: An English Rendering. Kandi: Buddhist Publishing Society.

Digby, Simon (1984). "Qalandars and Related Groups: Elements of Social Deviance in the Religious Life of the Delhi Sultanate of the Thirteenth and Fourteenth Centuries", in Islam in Asia, edited by Y. Friedmann, vol.I, South Asia, Jerusalem.

Digby, Simon. "The Sufi Shaykh as a Source of Authority in Medieval India",

Purushartha, vol. 9, 1986, pp. 57–77.

. "The Sufi Sheikh and the Sultan: A Conflict of Claims to Authority in Medieval India", Iran, vol. 28, 1990, pp.71–81.

Dughlat, Mirza Haider (2009). Tarikh e Rashidi, edited by N. Klias and translated by E. Denison Ross. Karakuram Books.

Eden Jeff (2018). Warrior Saints of the Silk Road: Legends of the Qarakhanids. Brill.

Raphael, Edwin (1992). The Pathway of Non-Duality, ADvaita: An Approach to some key-points of Gaudapada's Asparsvada and Samkara's Advaita Vedanta by means of a series of questions answered by an Asparsin. Philosophy series. Motilal Banarasidass.

Ernst, Carl W. 'From Hagiography to Martyrology', in History of Religions 24 (1985), pp/ 308–27.

Ferishta, Abul Qasem Hindu Shah (1865). Tarikh Fersihta or Tarikh Ibrahimi. Naval Kishore Press.

Frykenberg, RE (1986). Delhi through the Ages; Essays in Urban history, Culture & Society. New Delhi: Oxford University Press.

Gibb, H A R (2012). The Travels of Ibn Battuta. Goodword Books, pp. 210–11.

Gross, Jo-Ann (1992). Muslims in Central Asia: Expressions of Identity and Change, Duke University Press.

Gross, Jo-Ann and Urunbaev, Asam. Letters of Ubayd Allah Ahrar (2002) ISBN 978-90-0412603-9

Habib, Muhammad (1981). Politics and Society during Early Medieval Period (Collected Works of Professor Mohammad Habib), ed. By K.A. Nizami, vol. I, New Delhi.

Haidar, Maulvi Muhammad Nasir al-Din (1277). Suhail-i Yaman, or Tārīkh-i Jalālī. Persian MS. Muslim Sahitya Samsad, Sylhet. Compiled A.H. 1277 [A.D. 1860–61].

Hallaj, Kītāb al-Tawāsīn. Edited by Louis Massignon. Librairie Paul Geuthner, 1913.

Ibn Al-Athir, Ziauddin (1965). Al-Kamil fi al-Tarikh, Beirut: Dar Sader.

Jamali, Maulana Fazlullah Derwesh (1311) Siyar Al-Arifin. Delhi: Rizwi Press.

Juzjani, Minhaj Siraj (1873). Tabaqat e Nasiri. Translated by Major H G Raverty. London: Gilbert and Rivington.

Kabbani, Shaykh Muhammad Hisham (1995). The Naqshbandi Sufi Way, History and Guidebook of the Golden Chain. Kazi Publications, USA. ISBN 0-934905-34-7

Kaki, Qutbudddin Bakhtiyar (1310 AH/1893 AD). Fawaid Al-Salikeen. Matba Mujtaba'i. MSS: Bankipur xvii 1640, Ivanov Curson 413.

______ Dalil Al-Arifeen. Conversations of Khwaja Moinuddin Chishti. N.d. Lucknow: Matb' Hafiz Mahmud)

______ (1879). Diwan (Naval Kishore Press). MSS: Sprenger 453, Rieu Suppt. 238

______ (1890). Mathnawi e Mai Rang. Cawnpore.

Kandhlawi, Mohammmad Zakariya Muhajir Madani (n.d.). Tarikh Mashaikh Chisht. Karachi: Maktaba al-Shaikh.

Kashghari, Mohammad Sadiq. Takira e Azizan or Tazkira e Khwajagan, (Robert Barkley Shaw, The History of the Khojas of Turkestan (Supplementary to the Journal of the Royal Asiatic Society of Bengal), LXVI/1 [1897]

Khusrau, Amir (n.d.). Qiran us Sa'dain. Translated by Syed Hasan Barney. Dedicated to Mir Usman Ali Khan, the Nizam of Hyderabad.

Khusrau, Amir (n.d.) Afzalul Fawaid. Delhi: Matba' Rizwi.

Khweshgi, Abdullah (MS). Maarij al-Wilayat. MSS: Maulana Azad Library, Aligarh Muslim University.

Kumar, Sunil (2010). The Present in Delhi's Past. ISBN 978-818878443

Kumar, Sunil (2007). The Emergence of the Delhi Sultanate 1192-1286. Orient Longman.

Lahori, Ghulam Sarwar (n.d.): Khazinatul Asfiya. Matba' Thamar e Hind.

Lakhnawi, Abdul Hai Al-Hasani (1999). Nuzhatul Khwatir wa bahjatul masami' wa al-Nadazir. Beirut: Dar Ibn Hazm.

Lawrence, Bruce B (1976). "Afzal-ul-fawa'id — a reassessment." Life, Times & Works of Amir Khusrau Dehlavi, Seventh Centenary, edited by Z. Ansari. 119-131. New Delhi: National Amir Khusrau Society.

Maneri, Shyakh Yahya Maneri (1315). Maktoobat. Nawalkishore.

Massignon L (1941-46a). La légende de Hallâce Mansûr en pays turcs,' Revue des études islamiques, pp. 67–115.

Massignon, Louis (1982), The Passion of al-Hallaj, Mystic and Martyr of Islam. Translated by Herbert Mason. Princeton University Press

Nizami, K. A (1955). Life and Times of Shaikh Farid U'd-Din Ganj-i-Shakar. Aligarh Muslim University.

Nizami, K. A (1961). Some Aspects of Religion and Politics in India during the Thirteenth Century. Bombay: Asia Publishing House.

Nurul Hasan, S (2008). Religion, State and Society in Medieval India, edited and compiled by Satish Chandra, New Delhi.

Pinto, Desiderio (1995). Pir-Muridi Relatioship: A Study of the Nizamuddin Dargah, New Delhi,

Princess Jahanara Begam (2015). Mūnīs-ul-Arwāh translated by Dr Valiur Rahaman and Dr Mohammed Adil. First Edition: Jaipur. ISBN: 978-81-925848-8-1.

Qalander, Maulana Hameed (n.d.) Khair Al-Majalis. Collection of the Utterances of Shaykh Naseeruddin Mahmud Chiragh Dehli. Edited by K A Nizami. Bombay: Q Press (n.d.). Published by Department of History, Muslim University.

Raziuddin, Aquil. "Sufi Cults, Politics and Conversion: The Chishti of the Sultanate Religious Life of the Delhi Sultanate of the Thirteenth and Fourteenth Centuries", Raziuddin, Aquil, "Sufi Cults, Politics and Conversion: The Chishti of the Sultanate Period", in Indian Historical Review, vol. 22, Nos. 1&2, 1995--6

Rizvi, S.A.A. (1975). Religious and Intellectual History of the Muslims in Akbar's Reign, New Delhi, 1975.

Rizvi, S.A.A. (1978). A History of Sufism in India, 2 vols, New Delhi.

Saliba, Lwiis (1955). L'Hindousime et son influence sur la pensée musulmane selon al-Biruni (m.1048). Paris: Editions Byblion, 1955.

Sanaullah Mohd (2007). 'The Ultimate Reality in Islam', Proceedings of the International Seminar on the Concept of Ultimate Reality, IFFGRPR, Pune, and Department of Philosophy, University of Pune, 5-7 June 2007.

----------- (2015). 'Perspectives on the concept of basic elements in Islam', in 'The Cosmic Elements in Religion, Philosophy Art and Literature', by Kala Acahrya, Ignacio Arellano, Mariano Iturbe, Prachi Pathak, Rudraksha Sakriker (eds), Servicio de Publicationes de la Universidad Navarra, 2015. Biadeg. Biblioteca Aurea Digital del Grisco. 34. ISBN 978-84-8081-481-2.

----------- 'India's role in medieval Baghdad', Journal of the Indian Academy of Arabic. Aligarh Muslim University. Vol. 13, Nos. 1-2, 1990.

----------- (1999). Sabzwari ka Falsafa e Wojood in Quarterly Tahqeeqat e Islami, July-September, 1999.

----------- (2003). The Arab Legacy of Latin Europe. Aligarh: Samia Publications.

----------- (2006). The Arab Romance Parnassus. Aligarh Muslim University Press.

----------- (2008a) 'The Timurid Lyceum'. Proceedings of the Third International Symposium on Islamic civilization in Volga-Ural region (Ufa, 14–16 October, 2008), pp. 245–306, ircica, Istanbul, ISBN 978-92-9063-229-0

----------- (2008b). 'Beyond Hagiography: The Great Saint of Ajmer Khwaja Moinuddin Chishti', Proceedings of the International Interfaith Dialogue Seminar, organized by K.J. Somaiya Bharatiya Sanskriti Peetham, Mumbai, 4-7 Jan, 2008, pp. 337–66, ISBN 978-81-7039-272-9.

----------- (2009). 'Man, Cosmos and God in the philosophical summae of Islam', Proceedings of the International Interfaith Dialogue Seminar, K. J. Somaiya Bharatiya Sanskriti Peetham, Somaiya Vidyavihar Campus, Mumbai, on 7th to 11th September 2009, pp. 99–132, ISBN 978-81-7039-276-7.

----------- (2010). 'Elements of Yoga in Sufism', in History of Science, Philosophy and Culture in Indian Civilization. General Editor: D. P. Chattopadhyaya, Volume XVI, Part 2 History of Yoga, edited by S.P. Singh (PHIPCS-Centre for Studies in Civilizations, New Delhi, 2010. ISBN 81-87586-44-3, pp. 629–52.

----------- (2013). Spiritual Islam in South Asia: Aspects of Inter and Intra-Cultural Gnostic Sufi Mingling in the Indian Subcontinent', Proceedings of the International Symposium on Islamic Civilization in South Asia. Dhaka, 16-18 November 2008. IRSICA, Istanbul, 2013. ISBN 978-92-9063-260-3. pp. 179–95.

Schimmel, Annemarie (1975). Mystical Dimensions of Islam. Chapel Hill: University of North Carolina Press.

SGP (1916). List of Muhammadan and Hindu Monuments, Superintendent of Government Printing. Calcutta.

Sijzi, Amir Ala Hasan (1302). Fawaid Al-Fu'ad. Lucknow: Naval Kishore Press.

Simnani, Ashraf Jahangir. Maktoobat e Ashrafi, MS, Letter No. 73 (Maulana Aad Library, Aligarh Muslim University)

Smith, Roland Vivian (2005). The Delhi that non-one knows. Orient Blackman. ISBN 81-8028-020-9.

Spear, T.G.P (1994). Delhi, it's Monuments and History, Update and annotated by Narayani Gupta & Laura Sykes. Delhi: Oxford University Press.

Stephen, Carr (1979). The Archaeological and Monumental Remains of Delhi, New Delhi.

Troll, Christian W (2004). Muslim Shrines in India: Their Character, History and Significance, Oxford. Edited with an introduction by Marc Gaborieau.

Weismann, Itzchak (2007). The Naqshbandiyya: Orthodoxy and Activism in a Worldwide Sufi Tradition. Routledge.

SEVEN

South, East and Central Asia: A Dialogue of Cultures through Silk Route

Ranjana Banerjee

Introduction

Establishment of ties between South, East and Central Asia dates back to the era of the Silk Route. The route, created for promoting trade ties between these territories, became the stepping-stone for cultural dialogue between the traders, travelling through the Route, and the inhabitants, living along the Route. The cultural exchange thrived in the popular 'sarai' culture, wherein the traders, travelling for days and months halted in an inn along with folks from other races, sharing not only their own experiences, beliefs, customs but art, music, oral lore and national delicacies as well. The cultural encounter was initiated mainly through religious preaching. It's a well-known fact that a man's belief system primarily governs all the phenomena of his life—customs and values, ethics and aesthetics, the effects of which were visible in every aspect of their vision and innovation, art and architecture, literature and culture. Religion migration carried along with it, its various manifestations, adapting few features of the receptor in the process of dissemination. The whole process initiated a dialogue of cultures, leading to a confluence. It left an imprint on the territories along the Route. The innumerable exhibits of this confluence, the living remnants of Silk Route, are the silent advocates of harmonious dialogue between multicultural communities. This paper will focus on the various cultural encounters, which took place in the form of borrowing, adaptation, assimilation, dissemination along the Route, specifically South, East and Central Asia. It will study the commonalities and specificities traced in art and architecture, culinary, legends and tales.

South, East and Central Asia: A Dialogue of Cultures through Silk Route

The term 'Silk Route', coined by the German scholar Baron Ferdinand von Richthofen in 1877 denoted the trade route, which emerged more than 2000 years ago linking China, India, Central Asia and the Middle East primarily. It further extended to South East Asia, Japan, Africa and Europe. The route, created for promoting trade ties between these territories, became the stepping-stone for cultural dialogue between the traders, travelling through the Route, and the inhabitants, living along the Route. The cultural exchange thrived in the popular 'Sarai' culture, wherein the traders, travelling for days and months halted in an inn along with folks from other races, sharing not only their respective experiences, beliefs, customs but art, music, oral lore and national delicacies as well.

Historical evidence of the caravan trade along the route associates it to Persians of the Achaemenid Empire, early Greeks and Chinese and the Sogdians, the inhabitants of present-day Uzbekistan, known previously as Transoxania. The melting point of the different civilisation was Central Asia. The exact date of commencement of the Route is debatable; nonetheless, by archaeological evidence, the approximate time is considered to be somewhere between 2500 to 3000 BC.

The cultural fusion was primarily initiated through the promotional activities of various religious practices of the inhabitants along the Route. It's a well-known fact that a man's belief system governs all the phenomena of his life—customs and values, ethics and aesthetics, the effects of which were visible in every aspect of their vision and innovation, art and architecture, literature and culture. Religion migration carried along with it, its various manifestations, adapting few features of the receptor in the process of dissemination.

Buddhism from the Indian subcontinent was the first to spread through the Route. The Buddhist monks travelled together with the merchants, actively propagating Buddhist doctrines. It is believed that King Ashoka from the Maurya dynasty (273–32 BC) initiated the process of Buddhist missionary work, engaging several Buddhist monks for this cause. In the article "The Silk Route: Springboard of Buddhism in Central Asia", the author Tulsiram observes that the caravan of traders was often looted in the initial years of establishment of the root, so they preferred to be accompanied by the Buddhist monks, who were travelling to spread the message of Buddha. The saintly monks probably kept away the robbers (Tulsiram, 2004, p.63). The foundation laid by Ashoka was further strengthened and expanded by Kanishka of Kushan dynasty (127-140 CE) along the Silk Route. During his rule, the Buddhist sites were developed in the Bamiyan valley of Afghanistan.

Buddhism made its place amidst Vedic religion in India, Taoism in China and Zoroastrianism in Iran and its neighbouring lands. There are various views regarding the monk, responsible for popularising Buddhism in China. Some note that the monk of Kashmiri origin, Kumarajiva, born in the Buddhist centre in Central Asia (Kucha, 343 AD) propagated the doctrines of Buddha in China. He had translated numerous Buddhist manuscripts in the Chinese language. Many Buddhist monasteries emerged in China consequent to that. (Tulsiram, 2004, p.67) The other opinion holds that the Iranian monks introduced Buddhism to China through the translation of Buddhist sutras, evident from the scriptures found with their surnames. The translator used their home country as surnames (Kudara, 2019, p.98). Although this is a debatable matter, nevertheless there are no two opinions regarding the massive influence of Buddhism on the Chinese soil.

Apart from China, Buddhism had spread to Khorassan, Balkh, Bukhara, the Persian empire of Iran, through the Trade Route. The Uighurs played a significant role in the diffusion of Buddhism in Kyrgyzstan and Tajikistan. Buddhism had a stronghold in Bukhara, Balkh, Kabul, and Kandahar. The Chinese pilgrim Xuanzang provides a detailed account of Buddhist monuments in his work "Record of the Western region (646 AD). If the early period is marked by the tremendous impact of Buddhism, its art and literature on the socio-religious life of the people of South, South-East, and Central Asia, the medieval period is characterised by a massive influence of Islamic culture, its art, and architectural forms and literature on the lifestyle and culture of this region. The history of the Silk Route witnessed the dawn of Islam in Central Asia in the mid-seventh century. It was Islamic missionaries, mostly from Persia, who introduced Islam in Central Asia. Bukhara became the prominent Islamic centre. Gradually, Samarkand, Khiva and few other cities became the dominant cultural centres of Islam. The religion had a profound impact on the inhabitants of the Route. The most popular form of Islam was Sufism practised in tariqas—Yasawiyya, Naqshbandiyya, Kubraviyy and others. Its musical and mystical dimension made it appealing to the mass.

Islam was transmitted to China through the Silk Route during the Tang and Song dynasties (618–1279). The religion initially came to the southern parts of India with the Arab traders and thereafter had spread in other regions, along with the advent of the Turks in the middle of the 10th century. The Islamic preachers made all efforts to spread the religion, based on the principles of tolerance and equality, which were the basis of Buddhism too. During this period many Sufi scholars, poets and saints came migrated from Central Asia to northern parts of India. Religions like Hinduism, Manichaeism, Zoroastrianism, Assyrian Christianity, Judaism too left their mark on the Route, though their effect was not as massive on the Asian territory as Buddhism and Islam.

Confluence in Art and Architecture

Buddhism and Islam lefts its imprint on the art and architecture of the Route, and at the same time, it imbibed few characteristics of the receptive culture. The pagodas, the Buddhist shrines, the Taoist image of laughing Buddha from China, and several edicts engraved on pillars and rocks at various places in Central Asia are few examples of the confluence.

The unique feature of Buddhist art and architecture were the cave monasteries all over the Silk Route projecting dialogue of different forms. For example, a painting in the Dunhuang cave of China depicts the scene of an assembly of princes to express their grief on Sakhyamuni entering Nirvana. "After Sakhyamani entered nirvana, princes of different Central Asian states gathered to express their grief, crying, beating their chests, piercing themselves with sword or knives" (Buddhism and Its Spread Along the Silk Road, 2019, January 6). The scene reminds one of Muharram. It refers to the adaptation of Buddhist legends in Central Asia. Similar paintings were found during various excavations, carried out in Balayk Tepe, Ajina Tepe, Penjikent. Several monastic complexes, stupas, pottery vessels and ruins with Buddhist inscriptions have been excavated in Uzbekistan (Fyaz tepe and Dalverzin- tepe), Tajikistan (Ajina tepe), Turkmenistan (Merv and Kara-tepe), Kyrgyzstan (Chui River valley). The Uighurs constructed exclusive murals in Bezeklik Thousand Buddha Caves near Turfan. In recent past, archaeologists have unearthed a gigantic statue of Buddha (1.5 meters high) and a site of Buddhist temple near Bishkek, the capital of Kyrgyzstan. The eminent orientalist M.I.Vorobyova-Desyatovskaya rightly observes "Recent archaeological findings have shown that Buddhism and Indian Culture permeated every area of Central Asia, leaving direct evidence in the form of inscriptions and religious structures, as well as profound traces in the cultural substrata of the local people" (Vorobyova-Desyatovskaya, 1996, p.432).

One of the popular forms of Islamic art and architecture are mosaic works. The art form of the mosaic with coloured stones and glass originated around 4000 years ago in Mesopotamia. During the Islamic period in Iran, it was primarily used to adorn the walls and ceilings of the mosques. The uniqueness of the Islamic mosaic work lies in the fact that the stones were worked on with mathematical principles, depicting geometrical figure.

The other noteworthy art form is calligraphy. The Arabic form of calligraphic art, Arabesque was widespread across the continents. Islamic calligraphy was mostly used for adorning the Islamic tombs and mosques and in religious texts. It emerged from China, where the visual art form was best manifested in Buddhist calligraphy. Thereafter, it developed in other parts of the world. The materials used for the purpose were distinctive in different regions. Mesopotamia used clay; China used paper. Egypt used papyrus and stone. The Arabesque form used mosaic for embellishment. The motifs of Arabesque and the use of blue cobalt in monuments, traced in numerous Mughal architectures of India are the innovations of Central Asians. Specifying the various monuments of India, bearing the influence of Central Asian architectural form, the eminent scholar Prof Mansura Haider marks, "The colourful tile ornamentation and mosaic designs used in the Shah-i-Zindah complex at Samarkand had its replica in Jamali's tomb in Delhi. A striking resemblance is noticed in the square Samarid brick mausoleum (9-10 cent) and the square marble tomb of Sultan Hoshang at Mandu (15 cents). The tombs in Agra to bear a striking resemblance to the Central Asian monuments from Samarkand and Bukhara with Mughal calligraphy Arabesque and ornamentation with cobalt blue tiles. Some of the central Asian architectural patterns adopted in India are panjara, gumbad, jail, Taq, pasta, manara etc." (Haidar, 1999, p.83).

The interaction not only exercised influence on each other but also facilitated the two different cultures in evolving through the process of adaptation of various cultural trends. The modifications by the receptor as per the need of its time and space at times gave way to multiple fusions. The history of architecture exhibits several examples of fusion. The architectural form of stupas, as marked by Ahmad Hasan Dani, was developed by the Buddhists to preserve the holy relics of the dead. The original structure was a simple round mound, which gradually assumed the shape of a dome. (Hasan, 1999, p.8) The traditional Buddhist concept and architectural form gave way to the Central Asian Mughal monuments, the tombs with a dome, in a mark of respect to the deceased. The Turks brought along with them this form of the tomb from Central Asia to South Asia.

The mirror symmetry too initially used in Buddhist shrines in Central Asia (Buddhist monastery of Ajina tepe, Tokharistan) possibly was developed in Central Asia and later used in Timurid monuments. The Mughals brought the concept to India. It was very skilfully used in one of the Seven Wonders of the World, the Taj Mahal.

Architectural affinities were not confined to religious shrines and symbols alone. It is traced in secular art and architecture too. Radha Raina refers to the two architectural forms of roofing device, the 'lantern roof' and the 'Khatam band ceiling'. 'A lantern roof' is an architectural form of a roof that provides natural light into the rooms, whereas khatamband ceiling is an art of making ceiling with pieces of wood adjoined in geometrical patterns. Raina thinks that both the roofing architecture were invented in North West India and later carried through the Route to Iran and Central Asia. Other sources claim that Mirza Hyder Douglat from Central Asia introduced the 'Khatamband' ceiling in Kashmir in 1541. This form of the ceiling was equally popular in Samarkand, Bukhara, and northern India (Banerjee, 2017, p.333).

Musical Fusion

The cross-cultural dialogue found its expression in other fields of fine arts as well. Religion had a vital role in the dissemination of music along the Silk Road. Buddhist monks passed on the moral values through various forms of sacred chants from one part of Asia to another. Similarly, Islamic Sufis propagated their values through music, song, and sacred dance as elements of prayer among their supporters. The Buddhist Viharas, the Muslim Dargahs, served as the artistic hub. The familiar chants, songs, and instruments helped the pilgrims and traders to sustain in an alien land, and at the same time, they could not avoid the influence of the musical soiree they experienced in the course of their travels. Thus, the trend of Sufi music, or the style of Buddhist chanting, was traced in the music across the Asian continent.

Other than religious hymns and chants, secular music too travelled through the Route. Noteworthy is the significant contribution of Amir Khusrau, an offspring of a cross-cultural nuptial tie (born to an Indian mother and Central Asian father), Khusrau enriched the music world, blending Indian melodies with Persian and Arabic tunes. He is considered to be the creator of the ever-popular musical forms like Tarana, tappa, and khayal. Some of the most significant ragas, Yaman, Poorvi, Todi, to name a few, and the musical form of qawwali, is believed to be the innovations of Khusrau. He is accredited with the invention of Sitar and Tabla.

Amongst the folk form Chu-is, Shuo Chang, pien-wen, migrated to several parts of the Route, imbibing the local characteristics. The Baul music from Bengal carries the mark of Hindu Bhakti movement and Sufism.The musical instruments based on the depiction on the murals of Dun-huang caves illustrates various devices of Indian, Central Asian and Chinese origin—a Se (a long zither with movable bridge), pipa or lute, kong-hou (angular harp), Sheng (phoenix-shaped mouth organ), guan (double-reed instrument) (Chang, 1993).

It would be interesting to explore whether the lutes in southern Buddhist iconography from the first century, the ovoid lutes from North India as well as Central Asia, and the lutes from China are the products of intercultural dialogue or typological affinities. James A. Millward, an expert in the subject of music in history, believes that most of the musical instruments has been hybrid, which creates a cultural network, extending over regions and continents. Millward is of the opinion that Sitar, Sarod, Surbahar are further elaborations of the lutes (Millward, 2018). Though Sarod is considered to be the modified version of the Central Asian string instrument Rabab. The ever-popular Indian string instrument, Santoor is considered to be of Persian origin.

Analogous Motifs in Textiles

The textile motif, adapted widely by the weavers of the Asian regions of the Route, was the ornamental motif of 'Ikat', a unique technique of dyeing the warp and the weft threads before the weaving of the cloth material. The blurring or flickering effect, a characteristic feature of the textile, is due to the specific arrangement of each partially dyed thread. Though the universal term is ikat, the textile is known by different names in different regions. It is popular as Mangikat in Malaysia, abr in Uzbekistan, Banda in Orissa, Pochampally in Andhra Pradesh, Tai shi Kan in Japan.

The origin of the textile has been a matter of debate. A section of scholars observes that the design had originated in Indonesia or Malaysia (where the term is derived from) and after that was carried to other parts of the world through the Route. The others think that the pattern is of Indian origin, which travelled along with the traders to Central Asian territory. The analogous technique and similar pattern could not have been a mere coincidence. It seems to be more of an outcome of the established links between the regions through the Silk Route.

The other common textile motif is the pearl roundel animated figures traced in the looms of China, India and Central Asia. The place of origin of the motif is undetermined; nonetheless, the likelihood of the theme being transmitted by the pastoral nomads of Central Asia to other parts of Asia in the course of the Silk trade stands strong.

Some of the Central Asian techniques of embroidery, like zardozi and Tilla Kari, are popular till date. Close contact between the artists of the subcontinents reflects in the several antiquities excavated in the regions across the border.

Culinary Blends

Another vital part of the culture, showcasing the beliefs, is food habits, which migrated along with the caravan traders as part of essential commodities. As a result, one could find several analogous food items, in the menu of the inhabitants along the Route. The earliest record of the food carried by the travellers is the dumpling. On this issue, Holly Chase observes, "Turkic and Mongol horsemen on the move are supposed to have carried frozen or dried manti, which could be quickly boiled over a camp-fire" (Chase, 2000, p.81). The Chinese Wontons, Korean Mandu, Italian ravioli, Russian Pelmeni, Uzbek, Kazak and Tajik manti, Georgian and Azerbaijanian Khinkali are the few variants of the age-old dumplings. The fried wonton, samsa or samosa, undeniably were the modified versions of dumplings.

The rice-based dish, found in the different Asian countries with specific local variations in terms of ingredients and names is pilaf, plov or pula or the Chinese fried rice. The most popular commodity for trade through the Southern Silk Road or the Tea Horse Road (-ma-gu-dao) around 2000 years ago was tea. The terms used for denoting the beverage in different parts of Asia is very similar. It is chay in Persian, Hindi, Swahili; shay in Arabic; cha in Chinese and Bengali. The Route covered China, Tibet, India and gradually Central Asia.

Migratory Plots

Tales, plots and motifs too migrated down the Route along with goods, music, art and craft. The Jataka Tales, the stories of Mulla Nasruddin has disseminated along the Route with several modifications and adaptations. Justifying Feodor Benfey's theory, Nina Beguš analyses the six preserved versions of "The tale The Painter and the Mechanical Maiden" in four different cultural contexts: the original Sanskrit, Tibetan, Tocharian, and Chinese. All versions belong to the Buddhist canon, highlighting the significant distinctions among the different versions concerning their cultural and historical context and adaptations. She further tries to prove that the form and story of the tale are reminiscent of the Jātaka tales. The Tocharian version of the tale is included in a collection of Jātakas called the Pu⊠yavanta Jātaka (Beguš, 2018, January 12).

The scholars M. C. Joshi and R. Banerjee observe that the Jataka stories were a popular subject of presentation for the artists from India, Ceylon, Central Asia, China, Nepal and Tibet. The didactic stories exercised a great moral influence on the people. Several Jatakas and Avadanas depicted in Kizi of Central Asia are analogous to the paintings of Ajanta Ajanta. (Joshi& Banerjee, 1998).

Noteworthy Interfaces in Science

Indian works on astronomy were taught in China in the 7th century. During the reign of Al-Mansur (754-775), the second caliph of the Abbasid dynasty, Indian astronomers introduced the planetary tables and texts for the calculation of eclipses during their visit to his court in Baghdad. Several Indian astronomical works were translated into Arabic. The Chinese astronomer, Quran Xida translated the calendar with Indian decimal notation and arithmetical rules into Chinese, known as Jiuzhi Li. Abu Rayhan Alberuni's 's contribution in the field of scientific texts is quite significant. Alberuni visited India and studied Sanskrit with the sole purpose of reading the works Indian astronomy, geography mathematics, religion, and culture in original and translating them into Arabic. He introduced the people of the Indian subcontinent to the Greek, Roman, and Islamic doctrines. His book is considered as one of the most resourceful texts for studying the 'cross-fertilization of cultures' of medieval Central Asia and India. The Indian scholars bestowed him with the title of Vidyasagar, for his vast knowledge. The author of the article entitled 'India and Central Asia. Links and Interactions' refer to the various exchanges of thoughts 'the famous Bower manuscripts from Central Asia deal with Indian system of medicine' or 'Uighur texts found in Turfan deal with lunar calculations based on Indian astronomy (Kumar, 2007, p.18).

Translation of various Indian medical works into Central Asian languages, like Khotanese, Tokharian, Saka, Sogdian, has been conserved till date.

Assimilation of Languages

Together with the Buddhist doctrine, its form of expression, and scripts too circulated in the process. King Ashoka propagated Buddhism through edicts and inscription in different languages. Inscription of Buddhist sermons is found not only in Brahmi but Greek, Khoroshti, Aramaic. Similar edicts were found during an excavation near Kandahar in 1957. The Italian scholar Umberto Scerrato observes that the Kandahar edicts were not intended for the Indians, but for the inhabitants of the excavated region, which was under the rule of Achaemenians.

The excavated shrines, the monastic ceramic ware, and religious manuscripts bear ancient forms of Indian writing—Brahmi and Kharosthi. Scholars have even discovered fragments of Buddhist dramas in Prakrit and Sanskrit languages. As per the observation of M.I. Vorobyova-Desyatovskaya, "The Buddhist manuscripts found in East Turkestan and Central Asia remain the only original texts of the Buddhist canon known anywhere in the world. Even in India, none of these texts is preserved" (Vorobyova-Desyatovskaya, 1996, p.434).

Numerous Buddhist texts were translated from Sanskrit, Sogdian, Tocharian, Chinese, and Tibetian to Turkic language by the Uighurs and in the process, they retained many Sanskrit terms.

Many words used in the Asian subcontinent are derivative words, which travelled along the Route and assimilated in the lexis of the foreign land. For instance, the suffix of the names of various central Asian countries Uzbekistan, Turkmenistan, Afghanistan Kazakhstan, in all probability is derived from the word 'sthan'-denoting place. Similarly, the popular words in Hindi, like sheher, roz, taaza, meherbaan, khush, dastan, naan, kharboojaa, to name a few, are of Persian origin. Archaic Persian words are used in official documents of the Indian State of Haryana till date.

Similarly, several loan words from Persian are widely used by Hindi speakers and have been added to Hindi dictionaries, for example, roz, asman, taaza, khush,naraz, sheher. Undoubtedly, Urdu has played a prominent role in popularising the words and expressions of Persian origin in India. Extensive usage of Persian words and expressions in Harayana Police documents and Judiciary have been a subject of discussion in recent times.

In China, derivative words of Sanskrit origin are poli (polki/glass), mo-li (mallika/jasmine), cha-na (ksana/an instance), and many more. Of Persian origin are words like bāzhā (bazaar), bādànmù (badaam).

It is indeed fascinating to turn back the pages of history and observe the intercultural and inter-literary process of the Silk Route period. The cross-cultural links and cross-fertilisation of ideas opened a dialogue of cultures, leading to various convergences. The innumerable exhibits of these confluences, discussed above, are the silent advocates of harmonious dialogue between multicultural communities.

References

Chase, Holly (2000). "The Meyhane or McDonalds? Changes in eating habits and the evolution of fast food in Istanbul". In Sami Zubaida & Richard Tapper. A Taste of Thyme: Culinary Cultures of the Middle East (2nd ed.). London & New York: Tauris Parke Paperbacks.

Foltz, Richard (2010). Religions of the Silk Route. New York: Palgrave Macmillan, 2nd edition. ISBN 978-0-230-62125-1

Ghosh, G.K. Ghosh, Shukla (2000). Ikat Textiles of India. S.B. Nangia. A.P.H. Publishing Corporation, New Delhi. ISBN-817648-167-X

Banerjee, R. (2017). "The Living Remnants of Silk Route: Cross-Cultural Fusion Between India and Central Asia". In Rashmi Doraiswamy (Eds.) CENTRAL ASIA and SOUTH ASIA, Economic, Developmental and Socio-Cultural Linkages. (pp.328–40). New Delhi: MANAK Publications PVT.LTD. ISBN: 9789378314421

Hasan, Dani Ahmad (1999). Buddhism to Islam.Cultural links between Central Asia and South Asia. In N.N.Vohra. Shipra (Eds.) Culture, Society and Politics in Central Asia and India

Kumar, B.B (2007). "India and Central Asia. Links and Interactions". In J.N.Roy and B.B.Kumar (Eds.) India and Central Asia: Classical to Contemporary Periods. Astha Bharti. Delhi. ISBN-8180694577

Rossabi, Morris (2005). "Introduction. THE SILK ROADS. An Educational Resource". In Martin Amster (Ed.) FROM SILK TO OIL. CROSS-CULTURAL CONNECTIONS ALONG THE SILK ROADS. A Curriculum Guide for Educators. (pp. 3–8). China Institute in America. ISBN-0-9654270-9-9

Vorobyova-Desyatovskaya,M.I (1996) Buddhism. In Litvinsky, B. A., & Vorobyova-Desyatovskaya, M. I. (Eds.) Religions and religious movements II. History of civilizations of Central Asia. (pp. 421–48). The crossroads of civilizations: AD, 250,

Major, John (2012). Silk Road Encounters (p. 22). The Circle of Ancient Iranian Studies. Retrieved from https://www.amazon.com/Prehistory-Silk-Road-Encounters Asia/dp/0812240413

Berzin, Alexander(June 1996)"Buddhism Among the Turkic People". In Buddhism and Its Impact on Asia, Asian Monographs, no.8, Cairo University, Center for Asian Studies. Tulsiram (2004).THE SILKROAD: SPRINGBOARD OF BUDDHISM IN CENTRAL ASIA. In CONTEMPORARY CENTRAL ASIA .Vol. VIII, No. 1&2. April-August. ISSN 0973-5690

Millward, James.A.(2018). The Silk Route and the Sitar: Finding Centuries of Sociocultural Exchange in the History of an Instrument. In Journal of Social History, Vol. 52, No. 2, Winter 2018, Pages 206–33.

Articles by Two Authors:

Joshi, M. C., & Banerjee, R. (1998). Some Aspects of Jataka Painting in Indian and Chinese (Central Asian) Art. Across the Himalayan Gap: An Indian Quest for Understanding China, 173-81.

Chang, Lulu Huang (2019, January 10)) Cross-Cultural Musical Processes and Results. Music Along the Silk Route (From Second Century B.C to Tenth Century A.D No.1.ISSN.2191-6411. Retrieved from URL: http://www.jstor.org/stable /20796053.

Gasparini, Mariachiara (2014). A Mathamatic Expression of Art: Sino-Iranian and Uighur Textile Interactions and the Turfan Textile Collection in Berlin. (pp.134-163). In Transcultural Studies, an open access e- journal No.1.ISSN.2191-6411. Retrievedfromhttps://heiup.uniheidelberg.de/journals/index.php/transcultural/article/view/.../8711 by M Gasparini - ⊠2014.

Gasparini, Mariachiara (2016). SINO-IRANIAN TEXTILE PATTERNS IN TRANS-HIMALAYAN AREAS. In the journal of the Silk Road Foundation, The Silk Road (pp.84-96).Volume.14.ISSN.7153-2060. Retrieved from https://edspace.american.edu/silkroadjournal/volume-14-2016/

Kudara, Kogi (2019, February 28). A Rough Sketch of Buddhism in Central Asia, "Pacific World, Retrieved from https://chs.harvard.edu/CHS/article/displayPdf/3289.

Ashby, Caroline (1985). An investigation of Ikat weaving and warp printing and their application to contemporary design. Masters thesis. (pp. 411). Middlesex Polytechnic. Middlesex University's Research Repository at http://eprints.mdx.ac.uk/9858/

Beguš, N. A (2018, January 12) Typology of the Pygmalion Paradigm. Retrieved from https://chs.harvard.edu/CHS/article/displayPdf/3289

Koon, Yewan (2018, February 28). Crossing Culture in the Blue -and -White with Arabic and Persian inscriptions under Emperor Zhengde (r.1506-21) Retrieved from https://docplayer.net/30721966-Crossing-culture-in-the-blue-and-white-with-arabic-or

Zhou, Chunyang (2018, March 10). Buddhist Calligraphy in Ancient China by Retrieved from www.chinabuddhismencyclopedia.com/.../index.php?...Buddhist_C

Buddhism and Its Spread Along the Silk Road - Silk Road Foundation. (2019, January 6). Retrieved from www.silkroadfoundation.org/artl/buddhism.shtml

Cultural Exchange on the Silk Road – Advantour, 2018, June 10. Retrieved from https://www.advantour.com/silkroad/cultural-exchange.htm

Islamic Art (2018, February,12). Retrieved from http://lib.vcomsats.edu.pk/library/ADE212/ADE212_PPT/Lecture.../LESSON.%207Pptx

LESSON.6 .Unit 2 (2018, March 10) Islamic Art Introduction to Islamic Art. Retrievedfromlib.vcomsats.edu.pk/library/ADE212/ADE212_PPT/Lecture.../LESSON.%207.pptx

Music of the Silk Roads | Asia Society, 2012, September 26, Retrieved from https://asiasociety.org/education/music-silk-roads

The Sasanids, the pearl roundel design and its influence ... - Ghorbany

(2018, March 3). Retrieved from https://ghorbany.com/.../the-sasanids-the-pearl-roundel-design-and-its-influence-on-th

The art of Khatamband/ Kashmir Newz Specials (2016, March 5) Retrieved from www.kashmirnewz.com/story02d31032006.htm

EIGHT

Historical Bonds and Common Words Between Hindi and Turkmen

Meretguly Gurbanov

Introduction

The historical-cultural relationship and exchange between Turkmen and Indian lands is traced back to the ancient times. Although geographically apart, the people of these regions with different cultures, ethnic backgrounds and languages have been affecting and influencing each other. The land of Turkmen people in today's world is called Turkmenistan. It is a country Central Asian region. Some researches include into this region Tibet and Xinjiang (also known as Chinese Turkistan) of East Central Asia (now autonomous regions of People's Republic of China), West Central Asia with five former Soviet, and now independent, states of Kazakhstan, Kyrgyzstan, Tajikistan, Uzbekistan and Turkmenistan, Buddhist regions of Russia (Buriatia and Tuva) and Mongolia (Kablukov, 2004). But the term "Central Asia" mainly attributed to these five states.

As India (especially Northern India) is geographically not far from Central Asia from the ancient times till the British occupation of India there was cross-regional and social interaction which led to highly significant linkages. For many centuries, Central Asia was an immense reservoir of human energy and skills where many conquerors and many religions left their marks. Many great and world religions like Buddhism, Christianity, Islam and others were and are still present in the region. Huge treasure of art products, mosques, temples, guest houses, caravanserais and manuscripts were explored by expeditions and individuals. Many archaeological materials have also come to light in the excavations at Penjikent, Varaksha, Adzhina Depe, Altyn Depe, Merv, Gonur Depe, Jeytun and in the areas of Murgap river in the territory of Turkmenistan by Russian and Central Asian archaeologists. The writings of Indian, Russian, Turkmen and other scholars revealed the influence of Indian culture and languages in folklore, geographical names, moral-ethical code and other spheres of everyday life and rituals of Turkmen people and vice versa. Even the word Urdu comes from a Turkmen word "orda" which means "army" as it started as the language of army and military camps during the Mughals and Delhi Sultanates. As a result of these historical bonds there are hundreds of common words between Hindi, Urdu and Turkmen.

Historical relations between India and Turkmenistan

India and the Central Asian region share a long history. Central Asia's many expeditions into the Indian subcontinent made the way for a lasting exchange of goods and ideas between the two regions. New researches show close trade and cultural linkages between the Indian subcontinent and Central Asia, whose beginnings can be traced back to Bronze Age which corresponds to the Indus Valley Civilization and Altyn Depe, an ancient civilization of Turkmenistan. In those times Indus and the city of Puruspura (near Peshawar in Pakistan) formed major centres of Indian land routes to Central Asia and beyond (Azymov, 2018). Another research mentions that Indians started to use iron in 1000 BC and it was brought by Central Asian Turks (Khan, 2014, p.17). Historical documents providing information on Central Asia and its links with India are available in Turkmen, Urdu, English, Russian, Turkish, Chinese, and Tibetan and in some other Central Asian languages.

The Silk Route, the ancient trade route between China and the Mediterranean Sea extending some 6,440 km (4,000 mi) and linking China with the Roman Empire passed through Indian and Turkmen lands (Reconnecting India and Central Asia, 2010). A lot of cities were established along the Silk Route. In those cities Indians settled and lived their own life; they had their own social and political organizations, language, scripts, literature, art, architecture and religion. Historical records are evidence to the fact that Indian merchants also travelled long distances via Turkmenistan and the Caspian region to reach Kolkheti on the Black Sea (now in Georgia).

The current territory of Turkmenistan was cradle to the ancient civilisations, namely Jeytun, Altyn Depe, and Merv. The Turkmens preferred this region as their Motherland and built over 70 nations, from Ghaznavi Dynasty to Seljuk Empire and to the Ottoman Empire spreading to all corners of the world. The tribes could reclaim their territories only in the beginning of XVIII century following conquers of Genghis Han and Tamer Lane. They lived in the form of tribes and scrambled to build a single nation to fight against Bukhara emirate, Khiva khanate and Iranian shahs and Tsarist Russia.

India is known as one of the oldest civilisations with whom Turkmens had strong relations. As Mahatma Gandhi said, "India is a mother. She has two children. One of them is Turks and the other is Indian."The land of India became home for many Turkmen rulers, poets and scholars. Turkmens established many states in these lands. They established Kushans in 200, Akhuns dynasty in 450-550s (Orazsahedov, 2015; Khan, 2014, p. 18-19). Relations between India and Central Asia (Turkmens) continued during Mahmood Ghaznavi who belonged to Turkmen tribe Gaya and Delhi Sultanate times (Turkmenbashy, 2001, p.224). The spread of Islam in India is mainly related with the expeditions of Mahmood Ghaznavi (Gurbangeldiyev, 2011; Durak, 2000; Palabiyik, 2007; Karakuş, 2015, Raina, 2013). It is worthy and interesting to mention that in Telugu (one of the official languages of Telangana state), the word Turkolu, which means descendants of Turks, is used for Muslims. This is also proves the relationship of Indians and Turks (Turkmens) and it is used in this way, because Turks represented and spread Islam in these lands. After Ghaznavi dynasty (1186), till end of XIII century Turkmen commanders and emirs as Kutbeddin Aybegh, Nasyreddin Gubacha and Sultan Shemseddin Iltutmush (Eltutmysh) made important contributions in Turkmen-Indian relations (Orazsahedov, 2015). Between the years of 1290–1687 Sultanate of Halach Turkmens and Qutb Shahi Turkmens ruled these lands. Mughals dynasty which ruled these lands in 1536–1726 had important place in these relations (Kaan & Koc, 2012). The skilled scholars and commanders of this dynasty like Bairam Khan and his son Abdul Rahim Khan-e-Khanan highly influenced Turkmen-Indian literary relations (Orazsahedov, 2015; Schimmel, 1983, p.168). Turkmen dynasties re-ruled these lands starting with Ghaznavids ended in 1858 with Babur dynasty (Karakuş, 2015, p.III). Even though the founders of Moghuls dynasty were not Turkmens, still Bairam Khan and his son Abdul Rahim Khan-e-Khanan had important roles in the administrative body of this state (Gurbangeldiyev, 2011). At that time Persian language and literature were introduced to India. And mostly it has been done through Turkmen dynasties and sultanates founded here as they used Persian as their official language. Because of these many states, scholars, poets and other literary representatives of both regions were in close relations. Especially after the Mongolian invasion many Sufi scholars, poets and saints came from Central Asia and settled in Delhi, Kashmir, Hyderabad and other parts of India. They were under the patronage and support of humanist Turkmen sultans like Nasyreddin Gubacha and Shemseddin Iltutmush and continued to develop their literary works (Orazsahedov, 2015). India enjoys close, friendly and historical ties with Turkmenistan. Some edifices bear the Turkmen nation's name as in 'Turkman Gate' which was built in Delhi in 1658 and named after Hazrat Shah Turkmen Bayabani is a great symbol of the centuries old friendship. Moreover, members of the Khalji dynasty owed their origin to Turkmen tribes and military aristocracy comprised of Central Asian Turks at that time. They created a powerful organization called Forty, named so due to the number of its founder. India's major regions were also united during these timelines (Azymov, 2018). The researcher thinks that, this period and introduction of Islam provided substantial ground for sociolinguistic relations based on blending of originally Turkmen (Turkic), Indian, Persian and Arabic words which are evident in daily communication and he will later illustrate some examples. Kutbeddin Aybegh was one of the most famous Turkmen rulers who established Turkic-Islamic authority in Northern India. He was among those rare Turkmen rulers who were proud of his nationality. The proof of this is that, he left Persian and gave priority to Turkmen and his commanders were Turkmen (Karakuş, 2015, p.40).

Qutb Shahi dynasty (or Golconda Sultanate) also made important contributions to Turkmen-Indian relations. Sultan Quli, who was from a Turkmen family of Hamedan and received the title of Qutb-ul-Mulk in 1496, first served to the Bahmanis in the Deccan region in the South of India, became the Governor of Telangana State and declared independence in 1512 and established the Golkonda dynasty (Karagözoğlu, 2018, p.349). As other Turkic rulers they also supported poetry, culture and science. The founder of Hyderabad, Sultan Muhammad Quli Qutb Shah (1580–1612) supported Arabic, Dakhni, Telugu and Persian besides Turkic. He wrote poems in Urdu and Persian and had a collection titled "Kulliyat-i Quli Qutb Shah" (Karagözoğlu, 2018, p.357). If one looks at the lineage, it descends from Qara Yusuf Qara Qoyunlu dynasty which is of Turkmen origin. Moreover, naming patterns (Quli, Beg, Bibi) also evidence for the argument because such examples cannot be similar in any other Central Asian language. Ruhnama, the book authored by Saparmyrat Niyazov, the late president of Turkmenistan provides detailed information about its establishment in 1512 by Sultan Quli Turkmen, son of Ovez Quli Pir who is descendants of Bairam Hoja. Niyazov also points out to the lineage connection of Bairam Khan. In Farooqui Salma Ahmed's book titled "A Comprehensive History of Medieval India: From Twelfth to the Mid-Eighteenth Century" it is mentioned that: "Sultan Quli Qutb-ul-Mulk who established the Qutb Shahi lineage in 1518 with Golkonda as its capital was from the Turkmen tribe of Qara Quyunlu, which had the black sheep as their emblem" (p.177).

Literary relations between India and Turkmenistan

India both inspired and offered fertile environment for famous Turkmen commanders, scholars and poets while being source of inspiration. Many great Turkmen scholars visited and worked in these lands. Zia ul-Din Nakhshabi, the author of "Toti-name" ("Book of Parrot") was born in Central Asia. Al-Beruni came here, learnt Sanskrit and wrote Tarikh-i- Hind (The History of India). According to Karakuş, Al-Beruni came to India with the expeditions of Sultan Mahmood Ghaznavi, stayed in different parts of India, learnt Sanskrit and wrote a book on Indian culture and religions called "Tahkîk mâ li'l-Hind" (Karakuş, 2015, p.3). Dr. Mohsin Ali touches this point in his speech and highlighting several names who had great contributions in literary relations of these two lands. He says that, "Al-Beruni and Al-Khwarezmi were two well-known scholars from Central Asia who learned Sanskrit and studied India Sciences. Al-Beruni's Tarikh-ul-Hind provides encyclopaedic information about India. The prominent poets of India like, Amir Khusrau, Mirza Abdul Rahim Khan-e-Khanan, Mirza Asadullah Khan Ghalib, Mirza Abdul Qadir Bedil, etc., have links with Central Asia. Poets like Nasim, Nasafi, Maharam, Mushrib and Shaukat popularised Indian style of poetry in Central Asia. The Sufi philosophy of Maulana Jalaluddin Rumi found a natural resonance in the Indian subcontinents with its own traditions of Sufism and the Bhakti movement" (Ali, 2015). Abdurazzak Samarkandi also came here. Ibn Sina and Al-Khorezmi were acquainted with Indian scientific works. The move of Turkmen scholars to Indian lands increased with Mongolian invasion and many more poets and literary figures worked under the support of Turkmen sultans in India. They worked in their palaces and wrote beautiful poems. One of these scholars is Muhammad Avfi who first worked in Nasireddin Gubaja's palace and later in palace of sultan Shemseddin Iltutmush. His first book was Lubabul-albab and dedicated it to the wise vizier of Sultan Aynilmulk Fakhruddin Sharafulmulk Raziyuddin Abu Bakr Ash'ari. Muhammad Avfi authored many other anthologies like Javami al-Hekayat, which was dedicated to vizier Nizamulmulk Muhammad ibn Abu Sagt Juneydi (Orazsahedov, 2010, p.73). According to Orazsahedov, Muhammad Avfi was a great anthologist:

> "Outstanding scientist, historian and writer Muhammad Avfi while serving at the court and under the patronage of powerful Turkmen Muslim rulers, used the richest libraries of that epoch to produce his most valuable scientific works" (Orazsahedov, 2010, p.73).

During the reign of Babur, Humayun, Ekber and Jahangir such major cities of India as Delhi, Agra, Kashmir, Jaipur, Golkonda and Hyderabad became scientific and cultural centres of the region, they built libraries, madrasas, caravanserais and palaces. Artistic drawing patterns on ivory, wood, iron, as well as songs and musical art prospered there (Godarov, 2018; Karagözoğlu, 2018).

Two-way movements for trade and culture continued during Mughal rule and after that also. Alexander Burnes, the British agent, wrote that turbans of Punjabi white cloth were used by "whole of the natives of Bokhara and Turkestan" during 1830s (Kablukov, 2004). One prominent example is Bairam Khan (1500-61) from India's Turkmen region, descendant of Baharly tribe of Garagoyunly (also known as Qara Quyunlu) tribe who played an instrumental role through counselling and mentoring Humayun (son of Babur) to regain his lost empire. Bairam Khan proved to be a sagacious statesman and brave commander being also known with his poems in Turkmen, Persian and Indian languages. His son Abdurrahim Khan became a first rate soldier with 'khan of khans' title as well as a scholar. In addition, Abdurrahim Khan had epithet Rahimi writing poems in five languages, Turkic, Arabic, Persian, Indian and Sanskrit languages. He translated 'Baburnama' (Book of Babur) into the Persian language. His son Abdul Rahim Khan became a first rate soldier with 'khan of khans' title as well as a scholar. In addition, Abdul Rahim Khan-e-Khanan was popularly known as Rahim (Pande, 2010, p.98) and wrote poems in five languages, Turkish, Arabic, Persian, Indian (Awadhi and Braj) and Sanskrit languages. He translated 'Baburnama' (Book of Babur) from Chagatai (old Turkmen) into the Persian language (Pande, 2010, p.98).

Another prominent poet inspired by Hindustan is Magtymguly Pyragy. He lived in the 18 th century and is considered the greatest Turkmen spiritual leader, philosopher, Sufi poet and saint for his patriotic efforts to unite the Turkmen nation and envisaging current state territory between the Caspian Sea and the Amu Darya. Godarov also supports this view and he mentions that, "The Indian theme comes across in Turkmen fairy tales, legends and poems of such classics of Turkmen literature as Magtymguly, Shabende, Magrupy, Kemine, Mollanepes and others" (Godarov, 2018).

In one of Magtymguly's poems called "Bady-sabany görsem" (English equivalent would be "I wish I could see the morning wind") there are lines as the following:

'I wish I could see Hindustan in the East,
And Turkestan in the West,
And the land of saints – Rumistan (refers to Istanbul)'.

In these lines he indicates his strong desire to travel and see those lands. Pyragy's various poems are only proof that he travelled to India. He is describing India as the country of peacocks and the mythical bird – Phoenix. These lines are from the poem called "Ýaryň ýagşysyn" (English equivalent would be "The best of beloved"):

> 'The Indians were bestowed the best of lands by the God'.

Another example is from the poem called "Nurana düşmez" (English equivalent would be "Won't be brighter"):

> 'My eyes saw Hindustan, Iran and Afghanistan,
>
> The (Indian) Ocean, the Caspian (Sea), and Dehistan…
>
> You would not cover the distance I walked about'

The above verses testify the poet's travelling experience in this great country. He also mentioned the Indian merchants and talks of Indian desserts and red glass products among the best produces.

According to Kablukov (2004), there are about 250 manuscripts on history and literature of Central Asia, mostly in Arabic and Persian in the museums and libraries of India. Gurbangeldiyev (2011) also mentions that, "Turkmen scholars have visited India for several times with scientific visits. In 2005 they brought huge amount of copies of manuscripts belongs to Turkmen history from famous Rampur library. In 2010 in Ashgabat an International Scientific Conference titled "Bairam khan and Mughals dynasty was held". Khuda Bakhsh Library, Patna is very rich in this matter. Baburnama a book got compiled by Akbar has a lot of material on Indian and Turkmen historical ties. This is a great source for researches on Turkmen-Indian relations in medieval period (Kablukov, 2004). Turkmen scientists still make discoveries that firmly confirm deep roots of ties between India and Central Asia. Quite recently in Turkmenistan a treasure of 1515 coins of Vasudeva, Kushan king (III-IV a.d.), have been found. These coins are kept in National Museum in Ashgabat.

Impact of Socio-Cultural relations on linguistic development between India and Turkmenistan

The Indo-Turkmen relationship is pervasive and civilizational. These countries are embedded into each other's historical and socio-cultural attributes since time immemorial, vast, rich and diversified. "The philosophical, cultural and linguistic syncretism are the foundation of India and Turkic civilisations and the bedrock of relationship between these regions which finds expression in the lexicon used even today. The rules of Delhi Sultanate and the Moghul period were based on the civilisational synthesis as a result of the encounters between Turkic and Indic civilisations" (Ali, 2015). The relations between these two civilisations led to a unique blend of cultural system in all spheres of life – political, economic and social. New art, architecture, culture, science, linguistic values, new modes of exchange of ideas came into being which dramatically raised the levels and qualities of developments of humanity at large. "Hindi and Turkmen languages have profound impact on each other. Genesis and development of Urdu and Turkic lexemes in Hindi are the result of the centuries old Indo-Turkmen socio-cultural contacts. Hindi has a large number of Turkic, Persian and Arabic words" (Ali, 2015; Singh, n.d.). Our historical bonds have been translated into warm and friendly relations with India. For this, the trans-regional cultural ties between these must be comprehensive, and be alive to the demands and requirements of today. Turkmen state developed bilateral relations with India. Cultural days, exchange of delegations, scientific and creative conferences, opening of yoga and traditional medicine centres, statue of Mahatma Ghandi, Indian national leader showed that brotherly interactions are further being promoted. On the other hand, India established friendly diplomatic relations with the Central Asian countries, including Turkmenistan through following broad-based policy named 'Connect Central Asia' policy which includes political, economic and cultural connections between India and the Central Asia. The rising superpower country has an ancient and rich legacy of contacts and affinities with Turkmenistan as explained above. India considers Central Asia part of its extended and strategic neighbourhood (Mullen et al, 2014). Indian Cinema and TV serials are popular among Turkmen people. Similarly, Indian music also holds a special place in the hearts of Turkmen people. Hindi film festivals are held on regular basis in different cities in Turkmenistan. Turkmen cultural days are held in India in every two years (India - Turkmenistan Relations, 2017). India provides ITEC training for professionals and ICCR Scholarships to students from Turkmenistan. Twenty ICCR scholarships are offered every year. There are over 300 Students from

Turkmenistan pursuing various studies in India in various universities and over 400 Turkmen nationals have been trained in various courses through ITEC programme (India–Turkmenistan Relations, 2017). The Hindi Chair at Azadi University is functioning and 50 students are registered for a five-years course.

Common Words between Hindi and Turkmen

Turkmen is a member of the Altaic family of languages. It is classified as Altaic, Turkic, Southern, and Turkmen and it is spoken by approximately 20 million people, not only in Turkmenistan, where it is the national state language, but also in Iran, Afghanistan, Syria, and in Iraq. Turkmen language is one of the oldest languages and it was originated in Central Asia. And, it is noteworthy that the oldest inscriptions, which were found near Orhon River and which are in scripts used by Oguz are considered as the oldest scripts of Turkmen language. His Excellency, Esteemed President of Turkmenistan Gurbanguly Berdimuhamedov mentions that "Our mother tongue has taken its origin from Oguzkhan and it comprises the base of all Turkic languages".

Hindi (Urdu) is a South Asian language from the Indo-European family, and within the central zone's Indo-Iranian branch. It is classified as Indo-European, Indo-Iranian, Indo-Aryan, Central zone, Western Hindi, Hindustani (García & Yapici, 2014.) According to Reddy (2008) "In the 13 th century, language of India became widely known as Hindavi, Hindi and Braj bhasha and was written in Devanagari script. The name "Urdu" was given to the thriving language of this region in the period of Mughal Emperor Shah Jahan (1627-58)" (Reddy, 2008, p.290).

South Asia has seen emergence of numerous languages and scripts in time and space. Hindi (Urdu) today is the progeny of medieval historical past and enjoys the official status both in India and Pakistan. Islam came into the Indian subcontinent from north-west through Turkmen originated dynasties like Ghaznavi, Qutb Shahi and Mughals and Old Turkmen which already was effected by Persian and Arabic came with them. A glance into its journey suggests that since the beginning of11th century or probably earlier it was brought to use by both Muslim and Hindu population of undivided North India and was referred as "Ordu" meaning army in Turkmen language. Urdu language and literature suggests that it was largely spoken by the army and in the military camps and has words from Old Turkmen (Turkic), Sanskrit, Persian and Arabic. It developed more decisively during the Delhi Sultanate (1206–1526) and the Mughal Empire (1526–1858) periods (Khan, 2014, p.4). The growth of language is visible when Delhi Sultanate expanded south to the Deccan Plateau, the literary language was influenced by the languages spoken in the south, by Punjabi and Haryanvi, and by Sufi and court usage. The language was variously known as Hindi, Hindavi and Dehlavi. The earliest verse dates to the 15th century, and the golden period of Hindi (Urdu) poetry could be understood between the 18th –19th centuries. Lots of words from Old Turkmen language passed to Hindi (Urdu) language (Khan, 2014, p.4). Singh claims that, "While Turks (Turkmens) yielded to Persian words in matters of administration, poetry and social intercourse; they retained many Turkic words for military titles, weapons, military commands and organizations. Turkic derivations also exist in the hunt and hunting, also in terms expressing relationships and conduct in court among the ruling classes" (Singh, n.d.). Çöldemli cites in her work some claims on similar words between Hindi (Urdu) and Turkish. She mentions that:

> Purdil Khattak (1987) wrote a book "Urdu aur Turki kay Mushtarik Alfaz" (Similar words of Urdu and Turkish) published by Muqtedarah Qaumi Zuban. Zuban has listed
>
> 2608 words which are spoken by Turkish and Urdu speakers. According to Dr Syed Mohammad Anwer, from these 2608 words only 24 words are purely Turkish Words. The remaining ones are Arabic or Persian. So the claim is false that Turkish contributed to the formation of Urdu language. Also there are some works such as, Turkish words in Urdu in the Journal of Khuda Bakhsh Library, Relationship between the Turkish and Urdu languages by Jamia Millia Islamia (Alam, 2007: 31-56) (cited in Çöldemli, 2018, pp. 192–3).

There are many common words in these two languages. Some words are taken from a recent dictionary and given as follows (Naresh, Jepbarova, Muhammedova, 2017):

Hindi	Turkmen	Meaning in English
लबिास (liba:s)	Lybas, köýnek	Shirt
चाकू (cha:ku:)	Çakgy, pyçak	Knife
संदूक़ (sandu:k)	Sandyk	Box
छतरी (chatri)	Çadyr	Tent
तंदूर (tanduur)	Tamdyr	Oven
दोस्त (dost)	Dost	Friend
दुश्मन (dushman)	Duşman	Foe
वज़ीर (vazeer)	Wezir	Prime Minister
सुबह (subah)	Saba	Morning
ज़हर (zahar)	Zäher	Poison
लेकनि (lekin)	Lekin, emma	But
यानी (yaani)	Ýagny	Meaning
मुसाफ़रि (musaafir)	Mysapyr, myhman	Guest, traveler
अलबत्ता (albatta)	Elbetde	Of course
ज़ालमि (zaalim)	Zalym	Tyrant
सब्र (sabr)	Sabyr	Patience
सयिासत (siyaasat)	Syýasat	Politics
इंसान (insaan)	Ynsan	Human
दुआ (dua)	Doga	Prayer
इशारा (ishaara)	Yşarat	Gesture, sign
तोप (top)	Top	Cannon
नशिान (nishaan)	Nyşan	Mark, sign
अंजीर (anji:r)	Injir	Fig
अंबार (anba:r)	Ammar	Stock
अक़्ल (akl)	Akyl	Intelligence
अगर (agar)	Eger	If
अजब (ajab)	Ajaýyp, ajap	Wonderful
ताज (ta:j)	Täç	Crown

Conclusion

Hindi (Urdu) is a very modern language as compared to the original Sanskrit which makes the basis of this language. However, in the modern spoken Hindi, there are plenty of words borrowed from other languages including Turkic, English, Arabic, and Persian. While emphasising historical bonds between India and Turkmenistan starting from ancient times till today, through socio-cultural and literary relations, this paper tries to the commonality in languages also through above mentioned relations.

The main purpose of this study is to highlight a historical relationship between India and Turkmenistan through historical, socio-cultural and literary examples. It also aimed to show examples of common words between these two languages as a result of centuries old friendly relations.

Recommendations for further Studies

The new era provides an opportunity not only to discover old historical and cultural relationships between the peoples of Hindustan and Turkmenistan, based on archives available in these two lands, but also access the relevant material in libraries and museums around the globe that is unread and is waiting to be discovered. A scientific panel should be established to study and make research on the wider theme – "Relations between Turkmenistan and India: from ancient times to modern days". This panel should have scholars from both countries. They should study all the relevant manuscripts and other historical documents kept in libraries and archives. These new discoveries will serve in making the future relations stronger.

References

Ali, M. (2015). Concept Note. International Conference on Indo-Turkic Relations: Perspectives and its Contemporary Relevance. Jamia Millia Islamia, New Delhi.

Azymov, A (2018). India and Turkmenistan: Key Contributors of Security through TAPI. Paper presented at the international Seminar on India and Central Asia, New Delhi.

Çöldemli, S. (2018). Similar Words between Turkish & Hindi (Urdu) Languages in terms of the Open and Closed Class Morphemes. Karabük Üniversitesi Sosyal Bilimler Enstitüsü Dergisi, 8 (1), pp. 190–9.

Durak, N. (2000). Hindistan'a Kuzeyden Yapılan Seferler, ASAM Yay., Ankara.

Farooqui Salma Ahmed, (2011). A Comprehensive History of Medieval India: From Twelfth to the Mid-Eighteenth Century. Pearson Education

García, María Isabel M. & Yapici, M., (n.d.). Common Vocabulary in Urdu and Turkish Language: A Case of Historical Onomasiology. Pakistan Vision Vol. 15 No.1

Godarov, R. (2018). Turkmen neutrality and historical roots of the Turkmen-Indian relations. Paper presented at the International Conference "Science, Technology and Innovative Technologies in the Prosperous Epoch of the Powerful State" Academy of Sciences of Turkmenistan, Ashgabat.

Gurbangeldiyev, J. (2011, August 15). Dostluk ýollary: Hindistan bilen ata-baba gelýän gadymy gatnaşyklar täze Galkynyş zamanasynda täze belentliklere çykýar. Türkmenistan.

India - Turkmenistan Relations 2017. Embassy of India, Ashgabat. http://www.eoi.gov.in/ashgabat. accessed: 14.03.2019

Kaan, O. & Koc, B. (2012). Hindistan'da Türklük Müslüman Türk İmparatorlari Hümâyûn Şah. The History School, Number XII, pp. 221–33.

Kablukov, E. (2004). India and Central Asia: Cultural Relations in Middle Ages. Dialogue October–December. Volume 6/2. http://www.asthabharati.org/Dia_Oct04/Kablukov.htm. accessed: 12.03.2019

Karagözoğlu, B (2018). Persian Language and Literature in Golconda, the Capital City of Qutb Shahi Dynasty. Akademik Tarih ve Düşünce Dergisi, 5/16, pp. 348–61

Karakuş, Y. (2015). The Sovereignty of Turks in India in the XIII and XIV Centuries. Unpublished MA dissertation. Trakya Uniýersity, Edirne.

Khan, G.M. (2014). The Common Words between Turkish & Hindi-Urdu Languages. Master Thesis. Ataturk University. Erzurum.

Magtymguly (2015). Magtymguly: Collection of poems. State Publication Service. Ashgabat.

Mullen, R.D., Shivakumar, H., Taraporevala,P. & Prasad, K.K. (2014). Central Asia Backgrounder. Centre for Policy Research.

Naresh D., Jepbarova Sh., Muhammedova G. (2017). Hindiçe –türkmençe sözlük (Hindi-Turkmen Dictionary). Turkmen State Publication Service. Ashgabat.

Orazsahedov, D. (2010). Muhammad Avfi's works in India: A Brief Survey. Insight Islamicus Vol. 10, pp. 71–86.

Orazsahedov, D. (2015). Function of Anthologies Created in India in the Study of the Oriental Literature. Paper presented at the International Conference on Indo-Turkic Relations: Perspectives & Its Contemporary Relevance. Jamia Millia Islamia University, New Delhi, November 2015.

Palabiyik, M.H. (2007). The Expeditions of the Ghaznavids to India. Ekev Academic Journal 11(32).

Pande, R. (2010). Divine Sounds from the Heart—Singing Unfettered in their Own Voices: The Bhakti Movement and its Women Saints (12th to 17th Century). Cambridge Scholars Publishing. Newcastle. p.98.

Raina, R. (2013). An Ancient kinship: India& Turkmenistan. New Delhi.

Reddy, K.K. (2008). Indian History. Tata McGraw-Hill Publishing. New Delhi. p. 290

Schimmel, A. (1983). Hindistan'da Türk dili ve edebiyati. Türk Dünyası Araştırmaları, 24. pp. 165–72

Singh, K.G. (n.d.) Contribution of Turkic Languages in the Evolution and Development of Hindustani Languages. https://www.cs.colostate.edu/~malaiya/turkish.html. accessed: 25.03.2019

Turkmenbashy, S. (2001). Ruhnama I. Turkmen State Publication. Ashgabat.

Index